D0021514

Morale

W. W. Norton & Company, Inc.
New York

Morale

John W. Gardner

Library of Congress Cataloging in Publication Data
Gardner, John William, 1912–
Morale.
Includes index.
1. Social values. 2. Social ethics. 3. Moral
conditions. I Title.
HM216.G34   1978   301.2'1   78–810

ISBN 0 393 08823 5
1 2 3 4 5 6 7 8 9 0

To my family—all generations and all degrees of relationship—and especially to Billy, who wasn't here when the last book was dedicated.

Contents

Contents || 10

Acknowledgments

I thank Cynthia Hahn for exceptional help at all stages of the work. Every author knows the special gratitude one feels toward those who read all or part of one's drafts—often before the pieces make any sense. For such acts of friendship my thanks go to Elizabeth Drew, Jacqueline Goodwin, Caryl and Edna Haskins, Robert Meier, Aida Gardner, Francesca Reese, Stephanie Trimble, Harold Graves, and Gregory Vlastos. I also wish to thank the Ford Foundation for assistance in the last stage of the project.

Introduction

My life for the past dozen years has been wholly devoted to action and conflict in the political and social arena, and to practical work on concrete issues—from the improvement of education to the reform of election campaign financing. I have been wholly preoccupied with specific solutions to specific problems.

Now I want to step back and look at the motives that underlie social and political action. This is not a book about politics or social problems in the conventional sense. It is about the attitudes and values that make possible, or thwart, the regeneration of society.

It is only fair to warn the reader that I am embarking on a totally unfashionable venture: this book carries a message of hope. But it cannot be a message of blind hope, or of childish optimism. The grim world around us rules that out.

There is considerable evidence to support those who argue that human society is headed for destruction by its own hand—that having discovered nuclear weapons, humankind is moving swiftly toward a fatal and final holocaust. A century and a half of industrial development has brought ecological damage to a level that threatens the planetary environment. A steep upward curve of world population is coinciding with increasingly serious resource constraints.

Those are only a few of our more spectacular troubles. The nations are not working together to tackle these problems, partly because cooperative action on such matters is still in its infancy, and partly because all nations are experiencing internal difficulties. Everywhere the structures of tradition are crumbling; old belief systems are fading. People can no longer tolerate the old symbols of legitimacy. Often they cannot tolerate one another. Terrorist groups flourish.

There is no evidence that these problems will disappear soon. The world may face tumult and trouble for some years to come.

Humans seek to design social, political, and economic arrangements that will ensure the attainment of their shared purposes as a society. I have devoted much of my own time to such efforts. But suppose that our shared purposes are themselves in doubt. We can and should have differing views as to the solution of social, economic, and political problems. But suppose that cynicism and disillusionment destroy our will to tackle those problems, even destroy our zest in disagreeing. Suppose that people can no longer imagine that there is something significant they might believe in. First and last, humans live by their symbol systems. They live— if their society is healthy—by ideas that validate their striving, ideas that say it's worth living and trying.

No one can doubt that we face problems on this front today. Are there steps we can take to halt what appears to be a downward spiral of confidence and morale? To ask the question is to release a flood of other questions. What beliefs can sustain us? Is it possible to read the bloody scroll of history and still face the future with hope and resolution? Why bother to try?

I do not underestimate the difficulty of sustaining hope and faith in a hard world. From an active life in the public arena, I know all too well the case for cynicism and surrender. But there are things to be said. No one can provide final answers. I shall be satisfied if what I say here contributes to our joint understanding of the relevant questions.

It is especially important now for us to realize that just as shared beliefs and values are susceptible to decay, so are they capable of regeneration. The processes of decay are always at work, but so are the regenerative processes. This book is about the latter—a much neglected subject.

The reader will discover soon enough that I do not share the pessimistic view that humans are inescapably greedy, rapacious, and evil; nor do I believe that they are naturally altruistic and virtuous. Experience does not support a simplistic view of human possibilities. But it does, I believe, suggest that the only way to spare ourselves the worst in human nature is to call for the best. History offers ample evidence of the destructive power of humans; but it also records another side: it tells of a creature who is a stubborn seeker of meaning, a builder, maker, inventor, explorer—and a regenerator of value systems.

This is not a book about things and events "out there." It is about the attitudes and values at the inner core of your being. And no matter how private and unique those attitudes and values may seem to you, they are conditioned by your entanglement in the common venture.

Such matters may seem too intangible to affect the problems of here and now. There is a tiresome tug of war between those who say the only reason we're in trouble is that too many people behave badly, and those who say, in effect, "The only reason people behave badly is that they live in a bad environment." The first school of thought says, "Change people," the second says, "Change the society." There's something to be said for each view; neither is exclusively correct.

For a long time now I have dealt at close hand with the task of seeking practical solutions to some of the grimmest problems of the day. And I know that when you set out to accomplish change in the real world, you find that solutions may be blocked or facilitated by attitudes, values, expectations, and all the other intangibles that "practical" people shy away from.

Today a great many people are pursuing the search for morale and belief at an intensely personal level. One hears the troubled questions everywhere. "How can I find happiness? Quiet my anxieties? Fill the emptiness in my life? Think better of myself?" It is not my intent to pursue such queries in all their implications. But the reader will sense my conviction that fully satisfying answers will never be found in a self-absorbed search but only in a commitment to the human enterprise. I am not addressing myself solely to readers interested in public affairs.

We are living through a period of transition that historians will mull over in the centuries ahead. We don't fully understand it, but we feel it. Here and now—under the shadow of possible disaster—patterns of human social organization may be emerging that will prevail for many generations to come. The consequences could be grim by our lights; or, with luck, this could be a time of rebirth and regeneration in the history of the race.

Though I write as a native of the United States, and

my experience, insofar as it has any depth or texture, is limited chiefly to this country, the questions of social motivation and morale are of authentic concern everywhere. The species is in trouble. We must move toward some framework of order and shared values for the world.

Given the diversity of religious and philosophical belief—and disbelief—in today's world, no doubt the readers of this book will differ considerably among themselves on matters of faith. But people of all faiths, and those who acknowledge no formal faith, are afflicted today with problems of morale and motivation where social action is concerned. So I shall propose a way of looking at individual responsibility and social regeneration that picks up where deeper philosophical or religious beliefs leave off. I leave to my readers their deepest transactions with whatever they conceive to be the purpose or lack of purpose in the universe.

Morale

1 || Regeneration

Contemporary history displays our society suicidally
eating up its own mighty resources. Let it be noted
how the moral rot started, how standards were gradually sapped, then crumbled more and more omi-
nously . . .

These are not the words of a present-day commentator;
the passage was written by the Roman historian Livy
some 2000 years ago. And surely even then he was a
latecomer in an age-old tradition. No doubt in the Pleis-
tocene Era, some primitive, cave-dwelling father of the
tribe stared into the dying campfire and bemoaned the
collapse of the old values. There is no reason to believe
that he was deceiving himself: very likely the tribal
beliefs and values he knew as a child were, in fact,
fading.

At one time or another, almost all of us have emu-
lated that early father of the tribe in bewailing the

diminished vitality of the old values. (Even as we betray them, we bemoan their passing.) W. McNeile Dixon places some of the blame for deterioration on the human intellect: "I suggest to you that the most noble and potent of human instruments, the intellect, has one, but in respect of the concerns of society, a fatal weakness. It destroys faster than it can build. Moreover, it does not, and in its very nature is unable to provide the cement that holds communities together."

There is some truth in what Dixon says. But the human intellect that he finds so triumphantly destructive has been around for a long time now. If it has been destroying "faster than it can build" since the dawn of history, how did civilizations ever arise? Or the major religions? Or philosophy, law, science, and art?

No doubt there's something in us that moves toward "Chaos and old Night," in Milton's vivid phrase. But the human capacity to rebuild is fully as potent. All history bears witness to an irrepressible streak of creativity in the species, an extraordinary impulse to generate new values and regenerate old ones. Since our cave-dwelling ancestor stared into the fire, the human spirit has proved over and over its remarkable regenerative power. And our capacity to counter disintegration with new integrations is nothing other than the powerful—though not always prevailing—impulse toward form and order visible throughout the universe. Nature is vibrant with form, forms evolving, order dissolving and transforming itself into new configurations of order. I leave it to the physicists to reconcile that impulse with the second law of thermodynamics. All I'm saying is that Chaos and old Night haven't had an entirely easy time of it.

Rebuilding

Let me be as explicit as possible concerning my view of the human capacity for regeneration of values. Imagine that a thriving, lawful community were stricken, in the course of a single night, with an amnesia that erased every memory of law, ethics, tradition, and customs governing standards of conduct. There would follow, of course, days and nights of bloodshed and looting, murder and rape. The physically strong would take what they wanted. People would fight like animals over dwindling food supplies. Brutal crimes would be committed out of lust, greed, cruelty, and rage.

But the whole history of the race tells us that in a matter of days some members of the stricken community would begin fumbling for means of ending the terror. They would grope toward some consensus as to which acts were the most intolerable. They would seek to define certain limits that should circumscribe the behavior of all. And thus, slowly, painfully, they would set out on the long road back to the rule of law and a framework of values.

Each Generation Rebuilds

The example is not as remote from human experience as one might suppose. The lapse into savagery is never unimaginable where humans are concerned. The century that produced Schweitzer produced Hitler. Civilization is thin ice. The whole structure of values, beliefs, laws, and standards by which a society lives must be continuously restored, or it disintegrates. It will survive and flourish only if people continuously renew the values and reinterpret tradition to make it serve contemporary needs.

Civilized men and women are the products of society, but society is in the final reckoning the product of men and women: they carry within themselves all the generative capacity that has produced our laws, our customs, our values. Readers with strong religious views will say that God gave us that capacity; others will perhaps say that "Nature" so designed us. However one may choose to explain it, it is undeniable that in addition to all the other things humans do in the course of building a society, they always build a structure of values. Many of our contemporaries, heavily influenced by Rousseau (whether they know it or not), think that humans "in a state of nature" are not burdened by elaborate conventions, rules, and other consequences of value systems. But the anthropologists have disposed of that notion. Where human societies exist, value systems exist. In their deeper workings, values are among the binding elements that hold a society together.

Societies have not always agreed with one another as to the particular activities they label "right" and "wrong." But they insist on the importance of trying to achieve some definition.

In other words, we are not just the passive receivers of our culture but the active renewers of it. Thus our situation today is neither as bleak nor as unprecedented as it seems. From the beginning, each generation has been faced with the task of re-creating for its own time a fresh and living allegiance to fundamental values. Each generation—if it is equal to the task (and some generations are not)—rebuilds and regenerates the value system, reinterprets old values, and, more rarely, opens the way to new values.

Human beings are not without talent in the creation

of value systems and social orders. Indeed, these may be mankind's most distinctive products. In the world of living creatures, humans are unique in that they live not only in an environment of sensory stimuli, external and internal, but in an impalpable environment of symbols. We are the symbol-inventing, symbol-using animal. We elaborate vast structures of law, philosophy, science, theology, art, and custom. The symbolic environment, though its primary existence is in our minds, is as real as the objective world "out there." And it is precisely in that inner world that societies are created and preserved. What makes a collection of people a society is the cohesiveness that stems out of shared values, purposes, and belief systems. When the inner cohesion dissolves, nothing remains.

Today we need desperately to draw upon the human capacity to regenerate value systems; and we need, perhaps, a deeper confidence that we possess that capacity. In earlier times one generation might create patterns that several following generations would live by unquestioningly. It was as though one generation built the houses, and succeeding generations lived in them, forgetting their building skills in the process. Today we are more like people in a land of recurring earthquakes and tornadoes, where each generation must keep its building skills fresh and in fact rebuild almost continuously.

As a consequence of swift social change, humans today find themselves forced to make, on their own responsibility—without the secure support of long-established traditions and belief systems—the decisions that will shape their future. They are free to believe or doubt, to build or destroy, to choose the best or the worst. In a time of headlong change, no society can command its future unless it can in some measure impose coherence and direction on the forces of change. And that is out of the question unless the society has a firmly rooted set of values by which to judge where it wishes to go.

Those Who Rebuild

In the example I gave of the stricken community, the men and women who undertook to regenerate the society did so on their own. No one appointed them to the task; they were moved by some deep impulse to accept responsibility. And so it must always be. Some fraction of the population must commit itself to do what is needed: to reinterpret old values in the light of contemporary reality, and, where necessary, to forge new values.

Those who accept the responsibilities of rebuilding must do so not with a conviction that they are better fitted than anyone else, but because they believe that someone must step forward—not literally some *one*, but many. And the goal is not to find a neat solution to all our troubles but to move us forward in the task of rebuilding. The problems—in all their variety—will keep coming.

There is risk for those who take the lead in rebuilding. People who act and initiate make mistakes. People seeking the path to the future often wind up in blind alleys. Those who have the confidence to act creatively to regenerate the society must also have the humility to know the danger of overestimating what they can accomplish.

The Process of Re-creation

Most of the great world religions flowered in the period from the eighth century B.C. to the seventh century A.D., the majority of them in the first half of that period. Isaiah, Lao-Tse, Zoroaster, Buddha, Confucius, and Jesus all lived and taught in that era. It was in the sixth century B.C. that Brahmanism took shape. The epic period of Hinduism was the third century B.C.

It may be that once again we are entering a period in which we shall try—necessarily in very different terms, facing very different circumstances—to understand ourselves, our place in the world, our relation to "the great remembered dead," to one another, and to those who follow.

The older religions abound in accounts of creation. To dispel today's darkness, the seeking spirit must illuminate the process of re-creation.

2 || The Values We Profess

A comment is in order on the use of the word "values." Humans are so constructed that they regard some kinds of behavior as better than other kinds of behavior, "better" meaning more decent, more fitting, more deserving of the good opinion of mankind. If in a fit of annoyance I cut off your ear or burn down your house, you will believe that I have done something not just personally objectionable, not just illegal, but *wrong.* Presumably you judge its wrongness by some standard you have in your mind. When I use the term "values" I shall be referring to those standards you have in your mind.

Every society, preliterate or civilized, has gone far beyond such primitive examples to elaborate a complex set of standards of what is right and wrong, some of them written into law, more of them simply sanctioned by custom.

Many contemporary writers who deal with the condition of our society are reluctant or embarrassed to write explicitly about values. The reluctance is worth exploring. In the nineteenth century and at least until World War I, there flourished a narrow-minded, dogmatic, oppressive idea of "morality" that most twentieth-century minds found repugnant. This misguided zealotry gave us blue laws, Prohibition, the Tennessee "Monkey Trial," suppression of now-recognized literary classics, and other excesses. To make it worse, it was a piety heavily weighted with hypocrisy.

The twentieth-century style was forged in rebellion against that combination of zealotry and hypocrisy. Those of us who were alive in the 1920s remember the sheer delight of pricking the balloons of moralistic pretension. And skepticism toward anything labeled "moral" remains the favored intellectual style today. But while the iconoclastic style has prevailed among a certain elite, the majority of twentieth-century Americans continue with enthusiasm the old human preoccupation with what is "right" and "wrong." Consider the successful effort to outlaw child labor in the early decades of this century, the fight to give women the vote, the struggle to abolish the sweatshop, the long campaign against racial and religious prejudice. Consider the gas chambers, slave-labor camps, My Lai, the torturing of political dissidents. In all cases the issues are moral, and the appropriate reaction is moral outrage—but in deference to twentieth-century sensibilities the word "moral" is almost never uttered.

That background explains in part the reluctance of contemporary writers to deal explicitly with values. But there are other reasons for being wary of the subject, some of them sound: there are philosophical pitfalls; there are great dangers of oversimplification; and there is always the hazard of lofty generalizations that make people feel better but signify nothing. There are also some bad reasons for the reluctance to talk about values: such talk is unfashionable; it can sound naïve or preachy; and since everyone knows we aren't consistently true to our values, it can sound hypocritical. I'm going to set aside all the reasons, good and bad, and proceed.

Some Values We Profess

As examples I'm going to list a few of the values that are most central to current controversies.* The danger in listing them briefly as I do here is that one inevitably seems to be dealing in abstractions and copybook ideas that are far removed from the turmoil of everyday life. But it isn't possible, lacking the novelist's art, to portray adequately the battlefield drama surrounding the items listed. Values are not only fiercely defended but lied about, distorted, and flagrantly betrayed. They decay and revive. People fight and die over them; lives are ruined or ennobled; blood is spilled. Many people betray in action the values they profess. These are matters to which I shall return.

Meanwhile, let us ask ourselves what some of these values are. Remember that—despite the endless betrayals—these are expressions of the directions in which we appear to believe that ethical striving should occur.

We value justice and the rule of law. Of course as fallible humans we want justice mainly for ourselves, but commitment to the value is to be measured by our

*In these pages I shall limit my comments to the society I know best. But serious observers have pointed out that we must work toward some minimum common ground of values that all humankind can honor—no matter how distant that goal may now seem.

efforts to ensure that justice is done to others—not just to "our kind of people" but to other races and religions, even to those with whom we disagree. (Many years ago an old-timer who grew up in the Southwest in the 1890s told me he once saw on a small-town courtroom wall a sign that read, "Justice for Strangers.") The value takes on meaning only as we build justice into social institutions.

Justice is probably the oldest and most universally professed value. Anthropologists and historians are hard put to name a healthy society that has not honored (or professed to honor) some variation of the idea. Nature is unjust, humans are often unjust, yet we refuse to live in a world without the idea of justice.

We value freedom—freedom of person and freedom of expression, an end to all forms of subjugation or oppression of one human by another. It is a value as old as recorded history, though little honored in practice through most of history. Freedom of expression has come to have a particularly important place in our value system because we have learned that it is crucial to preservation of other freedoms. Shut off freedom of expression, and other freedoms soon vanish.

We value the dignity and worth of each person, without regard to wealth, status, race, or sex. To put it another way, human worth should be assessed only in terms of those qualities that are within the reach of every human being. In moral and spiritual terms, in the final matters of life and death, each person is equally worthy of our care and concern; and we seek for each person equality before the law and equality of opportunity. This does not mean commitment to a version of egalitarianism that smothers all possibility of individual excellence. Our concern is for the release of human potentialities. We are far from realizing the ideal of equal opportunity today. Indeed, we are still finding our way out of an oversimplified conception of equality of opportunity that once lulled us. For example, we once supposed that entering every child in school at age six was the epitome of equality of opportunity. We now know that by age six some children have already lost the race.

Valuing the worth of all persons has implications for human conflict: the most obscene cruelties of one group toward another are generally supported by the conviction that the victims are in some way less than human. Even Aristotle defended slavery on the grounds that slaves were "naturally inferior" to their masters.

The prevalence of war, hatred, and bigotry offers dolorous evidence of the capacity of humans for cruelty, hostility, and exclusivity; yet when we describe such behavior, we insist on calling it "inhumanity." The record suggests that such behavior is quite human, but something in us refuses to accept the verdict. Something in us stubbornly clings to the elusive ideals of love and brotherhood, values open, honest, compassionate relations and insists on honoring our common humanity, our commitments to the next generation, to the aged, and to the species. If we are to meet those commitments, we have a long way to go.

We are finally beginning to understand and value our oneness with the natural world. We are beginning to see humans and their natural environment in a relationship of mutual dependence. This means a richer recognition of our biological heritage and a heightened concern for our planet.

We are committed to the idea of individual moral responsibility. I am responsible for the consequences of my actions. Some will tell me that I may be forgiven my

misbehavior because of unfortunate events in my childhood, or because I live in an unjust society, or because
others have set me a bad example. But if I accept the
many paths of self-exoneration, the idea of individual
moral responsibility vanishes.

We believe in commitments and loyalties beyond the
self. In a community or nation that includes individuals
of diverse religious faiths and nonfaiths, diverse political and personal philosophies, there is bound to be disagreement as to the substance of such commitments.
The point is that we do not believe a life lived for self
is worthy of admiration. All true religion is a path out
of the quicksands of self-preoccupation and self-wor-
ship. Other such paths are commitments to one's family, to the community, and to the betterment of the
human condition.

One could list other values, but let these stand as
examples. Obviously we haven't lived up to them.
Human societies have never shown consistent allegiance to liberty and justice. But humankind keeps
dreaming of societies that will be faithful to these
ideals.

Where Are We Now?

Values do not emerge overnight, nor are they a result
of momentary evaluations of experience. Some are as
old as recorded history. The life of value systems involves both continuity and change. That is one reason
why, for the continuing growth and evolution of values,
the generations must mingle. "My fathers planted for
me before I was born; so do I plant for those who come
after me."

Some people believe that such continuities simply do

not exist today and that the decay in our values is far advanced. As they look about them, they see nothing but desolation and disbelief. In assessing that gloomy view, one must point out that we no longer depend so heavily on the chief device we once used to convince ourselves that our value system was intact—that is, hypocrisy. In an earlier generation, the sin was not in the doing but in being found out. Inevitably, the surface propriety led to the comfortable delusion that morality prevailed.

It isn't that easy today. One cannot recall a time when the disparities between values and behavior have been as freely exposed and fully discussed as they are today. That reality has had profound consequences for our time. Still, the heart of our problem is not that betrayal of values is more visible and more readily acknowledged today. The trouble runs deeper. The disintegration of traditions, customs, and communities has shaken our confidence. Our standards and guiding ideas are in disarray. We are confused.

3 || Keeping Values Alive

No rage is equal to the rage of a contented, right-
thinking man when he is confronted in the market
place by an idea which belongs in the pulpit.

THURMAN ARNOLD

If we agree that it is the task of each generation to bring
new life to old values, redefine them when necessary,
adapt them to the need and temper of the times, and
assist in giving birth to new values, we could do worse
than begin with Arnold's biting observation. It is a mistake to suppose that the solemnity of sermons and ethical discussions are the only (or even the chief) atmosphere in which values generate the vitality to ensure
their survival. Values live or die, gain strength or decay,
in the arena of everyday behavior—where greed and
principle confront one another in familiar settings,
where family members nurture or injure one another,
where ambitions clash and prizes are fought over,

35

where power is used or abused, where injustice is exposed or tolerated, where a virtuous exterior may clothe piety or duplicity.

Corruption

For reasons I shall speculate on later, commentators are particularly fond of Lord Acton's assertion that "power corrupts." Acton was right, of course, but power is not the only corruptor. A businessman may be corrupted by greed, a scholar by egotism. Hatred and fear and envy corrupt. The list is long.

Corruption may be said to exist whenever the true and generally honored purposes of a society or organization are defeated because participants who profess to share those purposes betray them for personal gain—in money, in power, in rewards to their self-esteem, and so on. The forces that breed corruption will be present as long as humans are less than angels, which will be quite a while if one may judge by currently available data.

Physicians say that germs are always around, and that whether one is healthy depends in part on one's capacity to fight them off. In the same sense, corrupting forces are ever-present. The level of corruption depends in part on society's equivalent of the body's mechanisms for warding off illness: its vitality, its morale, and the extent to which its members are committed to shared values and goals.

One of the strongest forces supporting corruption is the inclination of people to be blind to the particular forms of corruption that flourish in their own segment of society. To most of us, corruption is a characteristic of people we don't like. Corruption in one's own circle doesn't wear a corrupt face. Good old Charlie—your neighbor, your golf companion, your friend—would never bribe a legislator. It's true that as head of an insurance company he throws most of his legal business to the law firm of which Congressman X is a partner. And it's true that Congressman X is chairman of the committee that writes the insurance statutes. But if you think there's anything underhanded about that, you just don't know old Charlie.

One of the great attractions of Lord Acton's aphorism is that it denigrates a category of people—the powerful —who commonly excite envy, resentment, and hostility. It's quite easy, perhaps even pleasurable, for those of us who don't hold power to believe that those who do are corrupt. It's less easy to recognize that widely shared attributes, such as vanity, laziness, greed, cowardice, and self-indulgence, can also corrupt. In these terms your friendly pharmacist may be as corrupt as the most powerful citizen in town.

Another thing that supports not only corruption but every kind of injustice and indecency is the world-weary attitude of those who see it clearly enough but shrug their shoulders and say, "It's the way the world goes. What else is new?"

And then there are the large numbers of people who witness gross violations of justice or decency and disapprove, but are too timid to fight it. The shortage of heroes is chronic.

Anesthetized by cynicism or checked by timidity, people who are not themselves unjust allow injustice to occur and recur. The community long exposed to such recurrence becomes habituated and hardly notices it anymore—which explains the rage of Thurman Arnold's "contented, right-thinking man."

To talk about values without working to embed those

values in our customs, our laws, and our institutions is a hoax. Yet that hoax is such a common occurrence that hardly anyone takes note of it. All too often an accepted disparity between the values we profess and the actions we take becomes embedded in our customs and institutions. If we are to be true to ourselves, we must strive to change our institutional arrangments to conform to what we say we believe. And most people find that a downright aggravating task. As a nation we managed to live for eighty-nine years with the phrase "all men are created equal" before we freed the slaves. And we let another fifty-five years pass before we gave women the vote. We don't rush into these things.

The first simple (but perilously difficult) requirement of a living value system is that people act in behalf of their values. But humans have always preferred to pay homage to their values in ritual and pious proclamation. Hence the social usefulness of those irrepressible spirits who defy the community's habituation and speak against injustice or corruption or dehumanization. There must be a Joseph Welch to stand up to a Joe McCarthy. There must be a Rosa Parks to sit in the front of the bus. There must be plain words and symbolic acts that make values real in action.

I don't wish to focus attention solely on those values that produce confrontation and drama. A society's values are also reflected in innumerable quiet acts: generosity toward a stranger, loving care for an invalid, strength in adversity.

The Grand Inquisitor

There are—to oversimplify—two sharply conflicting ways of reacting to the gap between aspiration and

performance in the realm of values. One says, "Close
the gap by bringing performance closer to aspiration.
Make people better!" The other says, "The gap reflects
something unchangeable in human nature. Accept it
and act accordingly." Exemplifying the latter view are
the newspaper, movie, and television executives who
feel perfectly justified in enriching themselves by playing to the people's lowest impulses. "It's what the public wants" is the standard justification. Many politicians
have no qualms about playing upon the least admirable
prejudices and hatreds of their constitutents. "Would
you deny that the prejudices are there?" they might
ask. "Are we not supposed to represent our people?"

Are such "realistic" arguments acceptable? One cannot comfortably answer yes; yet we couldn't live with
media people and politicians who forced on us what
they considered morally right for us. So the answers
aren't easy; they aren't supposed to be. Yet, accepting
all the complexities of the question, one can argue that
we have a duty to approach people with a sense of what
they can be at their best, knowing that by so doing one
may heighten the likelihood of their reaching for the
best.

This is wholly at odds with the view of the Grand
Inquisitor in Dostoevsky's *The Brothers Karamazov.*
The Grand Inquisitor accused Jesus of overestimating
human capacity for spiritual strength and of setting
standards so high that they could be met by no more
than a small group of the elect. "I swear, man is weaker
and baser by nature than Thou has believed him! . . .
Thou didst ask too much of him. . . . Respecting him less,
Thou wouldst have asked less of him. That would have
been more like love, for his burden would have been
lighter."

The Grand Inquisitor, who sees humans as "weak,

vicious, worthless, and rebellious," explains to Jesus, "We have corrected Thy work." His formula is starkly simple: proceed on the assumption that humans are children; keep them under heavy discipline; make them happy by sparing them the burdens of freedom.

Those who embrace religious or political systems based on individual moral responsibility cannot accept the Grand Inquisitor's formulation of the problem, much less his conclusion. Clearly there are elements in human nature antagonistic to high standards; but there is also an element in human nature that *sets those high standards* and seeks to meet them. The Grand Inquisitor's strategy prejudges the outcome, expects the worst, and creates social arrangements that seek to put a lid on human possibilities.

Ironically, it is not solely by moral criteria that the Grand Inquisitor's argument appears defective. If treating people like children really made them happy, no extraordinary force would be needed. But every contemporary example suggests that the ruler who sets out to treat his subjects as children needs quite a few machine guns. Evidently some of the children are reluctant to accept the arrangement.

4 || The Lifeline of the Race

The most powerful moving forces in history are not societies—which are forever decaying—but highly motivated people and their ideas of what is worth living for and striving for.

Every year tens of millions of Americans come to the nation's capital to visit our national shrines. Day after day one sees them streaming through the Lincoln Memorial, the Washington Monument, the Capitol. But the spirit of the nation does not reside in the physical structures. It is in the minds of the citizens who come to look at the structures. That is where a vital society begins; and, if it ends, that is where it ends. If they stop believing, if they lose faith, if they stop caring, the monuments will be meaningless piles of stone, and the nation will be as lifeless as the stones. There will still be the land and a lot of people milling around; but the venture that began with the Declaration of Independence, the venture familiarly known as America, will be dead.

It need not happen. But it could. The task of the moment is to re-create a motivated society. If we fail in that, forget the rest. When a society disintegrates, you may be sure that its animating ideas and ideals died first in the minds of men and women.

The Unknowable Future

A Chinese proverb says, "To prophesy is extremely difficult—especially with respect to the future." A nineteenth-century horse breeder foresaw the day when transportation would be wholly revolutionized by the breeding of a horse that could run at a pace of fifty miles an hour indefinitely. The Wright brothers thought that invention of the airplane would bring an end to all wars, because under observation from the air no military force could maneuver secretly.

If it's hard to know the shape of things to come, it's virtually impossible to design social arrangements for that unknown future. It is tempting to imagine that we can draw neat blueprints of a society that will serve future generations, but we cannot. This truth is ignored to the point of comedy by many of the earnest voices that tell us how to reconstruct our society. There's a chronic shortage of people who can solve our problems here and now, but never a shortage of people who will tell us how to design our society for an unpredictable future. They woefully underestimate the imponderables of social change, especially now, when its swift flow threatens the continuities of human experience in ways we can hardly imagine.

We cannot design today the institutions for a future we cannot foretell. The best we can do is to foster the kinds of men and women who can cope with the future as it unfolds, who are capable of facing new realities as they emerge without forgetting the continuities in our tradition and our longer-term aspirations as a free people. If we are to create a society for the transitions ahead that is worthy of our heritage of freedom, our surest resource will be men and women of courage and conviction who carry within themselves a sense of what is important for the human future, a sense of what makes societies vital and humane.

A System That Evolves

With the old ways losing their hold and new ways yet to be shaped, it will be useful to remember that the time-honored customs and arrangements of a society—its institutions—have never been the solid foundation that they are widely assumed to be. They are creations of the human mind, forever changing.

We might find contemporary changes less disturbing if we reflected on the profound transformations that have already occurred in our own history. When the British colonized North America, they assumed that they could transport their institutions and attitudes to these shores more or less intact; but before the seventeenth century ended, the North American colonists had created a strikingly new way of life. They had developed attitudes and social arrangements that made the Revolution almost inevitable. That was the first America. It wasn't born in 1776; that's when it was old enough to leave home. It underwent marked changes, particularly with the emergence of Jacksonian democracy, but from beginning to end it was rural, essentially preindustrial, overwhelmingly Protestant, and relatively insulated from the rest of the world. Then in the mid-nineteenth century the first America slowly disappeared; and a very different society took shape as the powerful stirrings of industrialism began their transforming work. The second America was increasingly urban, secular, industrial, heavily salted with immigrants, pursuing ardently the revolutions in communication and transportation, and immensely exhilarated by its own growth. The third America, which came in with Franklin D. Roosevelt, was acutely conscious of social issues and committed to use the power of the federal government to resolve those issues. It was also internationalist and—ultimately—enormously preoccupied with the arts of war. (I have sketched the three Americas in grossly oversimplified terms, but the reader will recognize the underlying reality of profound social change.)

Now we are undergoing another transition. We cannot know what the next America will be like; but no one who reflects on the profound alterations—economic, political, and social—that accompanied past transitions can doubt that "the American system"—so often piously regarded as immutable—is in fact changing continuously, all the while retaining powerful continuities of character and spirit.

The Lifeline of the Race

It isn't enough to tell people that they must be equal to the challenges the future will bring. The contemporary mind asks, "Why? What makes it worthwhile? What can I believe? What can I admire and take sustenance from?"

The question isn't easily answered. Around the individual today swirls a bewildering jumble of faiths, heresies, and unbelief. It's hard for any thoughtful person to observe, in Cardinal Newman's words, "the defeat of good, the success of evil . . . the pervading idolatries, the corruptions" and still find ground for moral striving.

It isn't only the modern mind that has had difficulty with such questions. More than 2000 years ago, Ecclesiastes, who had a boundless capacity to be disappointed by the world, was particularly troubled that one cannot expect just rewards in this life. It concerned him that the wise man fares no better than the fool, the righteous no better than the wicked. The race is not to the swift: "Time and chance happeneth to them all."

It is true that there is no assurance of reward for effort or wisdom or talent or virtue, at least not in the terms that the world commonly reckons rewards— money, status, acclaim, pleasure, or power. Sensible people grasp that reality fairly early.

So why bother to meet any standards of behavior? Why strive to diminish human suffering? Why combat injustice? For some the answer may lie in being true to their religious convictions; for others, in expressing their allegiance to a moral order (however they may conceive it); for still others, simply in trying to be true to what humans can be at their best.

"Trying to be true to what humans can be at their best." The words are deceptively simple, but the idea has great power. Humans have shown themselves capable of degradation as well as nobility, of cruelty as well as kindness, of greed as well as generosity. To pretend that the darker side of human nature dissolves under the cleansing rays of idealism is to delude oneself. Yet even in those moments of history when corruption and degradation seemed wholly triumphant, there were some men and women who continued stubbornly to seek justice and liberty and a world that honored the worth and dignity of each person; there were those who strove for excellence; there were those who tried to create a more humane environment for those around them. Some left their names in the history books, others were well known in their time and place but are unknown to us; and some were perhaps never heard of beyond their neighborhood. You have known such people. Some have bettered the lives of millions of persons, others may have helped only a few among their immediate family and friends. It doesn't matter.

An enduring basis for moral commitment is to affirm our allegiance to those men and women, to associate ourselves with the human spirit striving for the best. To remind ourselves that they existed, is a message of solidarity for every seriously striving person.

There is no evidence that humans can perfect themselves or their societies. But their impulse to try accounts for the best moments in humankind's stormy history. People of various religious and philosophical views explain the impulse in varying terminology, but few deny that it exists. The impulse may be layered over, ignored, or smothered by worldliness and cynicism; but it is there—and, in some people, inextinguishable. We draw our spiritual strength from just those people, even though most of them are unknown to us. They are the bearers of the spirit, the lifeline of the race, stretching back through the centuries.

Continuities of the Spirit

All of us celebrate our values in our behavior. The way we act and conduct our lives says something to others —perhaps something reprehensible, perhaps something encouraging. We are teaching by example—bad lessons or good. Each of us is saying,—in our behavior — "This is one thing of which humankind is capable." We are allying ourselves with those who have exalted humankind or with those who have degraded it. All those who set standards for themselves, rear their children responsibly, strengthen the bonds of community, do their work creditably and accept individual responsibility are building the common future. It is the universal ministry.

This is a heartening truth for those people who wish to assist in the regeneration of values but can't imagine how they can possibly influence this huge and complex society. They are not as powerless as they believe. No one can measure the contagion of ideas, values, and aspirations as expressed in the lives and acts of individual men and women. That contagion produces continuities in social behavior that are not readily discernible. We are familiar with the continuities evident in the influence of great teachers, prophets, and philosophers, but we have given little thought to the moral and spiritual lineage of everyday human interaction. We couldn't possibly name the many people who have influenced us, sometimes through a single exemplary act. As they influenced us, others influenced them. Those living today will influence others. The web of influence reaches back through the generations, stretching over centuries a skein of incomparable delicacy and strength. That moral and spiritual lineage, often preserved at great cost, is an antidote to the cynicism so often generated by the contemporary inflated self, which seeks all meaning in its own aches and itches.

5 || A New Vision

When people talk about the decay of values, one occasionally hears it said that we need "a new vision." I do not feel at home with the phrase. I recognize that those who use it feel a genuine hunger; but it may be that they are looking for something they can never find, at least not in a form they would recognize.

It would suit the style of this self-conscious, programmatic, word-and-number saturated age to come across something in print, formally entitled *A New Vision*, which would rationally set forth assumptions, values, principles, and recommendations: a motorist's map of the journey ahead, complete with mileages.

We shall never find it. And even if we were to find it, it would be too sterile to nourish anyone.

The Way to the Enchanted Forest

Consider the story of the old forester who was said to be the only person who knew the way to the Enchanted

Forest. In the forest, according to legend, beauty was in every rock and tree and stream; the deer approached humans without fear; sun and shadow, earth and sky, the sounds and stillness of the forest all combined to give the visitor a sense of exaltation and clear vision. Every year people visited the old man to ask the way to the forest, but he answered in what seemed to them to be irrelevancies. To some he said, "I'll teach you the ways of the birds and wild animals"; but that didn't satisfy them. Or he would say, "I'll teach you how to live off the land, to find water where no one else can find it, to find shelter from the cold, to find food"; but that didn't interest them either. Sometimes he said, "I'll teach you the ways of the nature person: patience, endurance, seeing, listening, being a part of nature." His offers satisfied no one.

When the old man died, his daughter married a young man who knew the whole area well, and one day he said to her, "Isn't it true that there is no Enchanted Forest?"

"Not as a place on the map," she said.

"Why didn't your father tell his visitors that?"

"Because he was stubborn. If they had let him teach them the ways of nature, they would have discovered the only enchanted forest there is. It has many locations but few discoverers."

Visions and Self-Regard

We've learned that the more extravagant visions—of society perfected, of humankind purged of flaws—not only produce disillusionment but, by their very extravagance, belittle the hard, unglamorous, everyday efforts of serious people to make the world better. And they set the stage for those who say, "First you have to destroy this wicked society, and then build the dream."

Yet—short of such flights of fancy—we do need visions and visionaries. The relentless pressure of each succeeding day, the incessant battering of life, absorbs our energies and shortens our perspective. We need to be reminded of larger and longer-term goals. We need to preserve our sense of direction.

But what we need is not simply a vision of the goal but a vision of ourselves moving toward it, as *capable* of moving toward it, as finding our fulfillment in moving toward it. We have to see ourselves, *feel* ourselves as capable of the necessary exertions. And such morale is possible only if we have a reasonably positive feeling about the striving and achieving we've already done, not denying the failures, but taking strength from the gains. Surely our long struggles to protect our freedoms, to establish racial justice, to fight corruption, to prevent economic exploitation—surely these and so many other struggles have taught us that what counts is staying power. And why have we stayed with such tasks? Because to do so has always been inextricably tied up with our sense of ourselves. We could not have ceased striving and still preserve our self-regard.

Evidently, then, a vision is only significant to the extent that it is linked to our conscious and unconscious sense of our own character and destiny. If we arrive at "a new vision" for an endangered planet, suitable for a world rudely separated from long-held traditions, a vision that will lift us out of our hopelessness and lack of faith, it will have such roots. And only portions of it will be expressible in words. Whitehead said, ". . . human life is driven forward by the dim apprehension of notions too general for its existing language." The expository sentence is only one—and probably not the best— way of expressing a vision that people can live by. No doubt the words of the Declaration of Independence and the Constitution are extremely important, but for most Americans, the vision that brought us through two centuries with enormous vigor has involved far more than words. It is compounded of shared memories and hopes, things rational and irrational, continuity and evolution, a sense of place, symbols, a history, dreams, an ingrained way of looking at our life together. And it has never been static; it has evolved, unfolded, changed, ripened, deepened.

Compared with Europeans, we have been irreverent toward tradition. Yet with every decade, from the beginning, our sense of ourselves has been given texture by an ever-deeper sense of our land and our past. Slowly—deeper than words—the images, symbols, and memories accumulated: the struggle for independence, the beckoning excitement of a continent to be settled, the wide Missouri, the gold rush, the underground railway, the face of Lincoln, sod houses on the prairie, the Little Bighorn, Ellis Island, immigrant neighborhoods, the American Expeditionary Force, the Model T, breadlines, Pearl Harbor, the affluent society, the Peace Corps, Vietnam. Good memories and heartbreaking memories. Growth and tragedy. Lessons learned and lessons still to learn.

The vision we started with had a past. Despite the colonial American's sense of a fresh start and a new slate to write on, we drew deeply on the European tradition. So it will be with any vision we fashion today: the new will grow organically out of the old. We shall build it over years. Some of it will be expressed in words, some of it in symbolic acts and memorable deeds. It will be compounded of hopes, memories, aspirations, estimates of reality, dreams—some of which can never be put into words.

Today we are moving toward a vision that is more mature than any that most of us have held in the past. With due respect to our forebears, particularly those of our second century as a nation, it must be said that many of them were sustained by a view of the future that said insistently, "More . . . bigger . . . richer . . . happier." It was the dream of moving inexorably onward and upward. Coming into focus now is an infinitely more complex future in which there are real constraints, in which we understand that our own fallibility is part of the problem, in which the voyage is as important as the destination.

A good many people understand today that the new vision is going to have to be inclusive, big enough for everybody. It isn't enough for the businessman to envisage a future that would be perfect for businessmen; nor union leaders for labor; nor professors for the university. We must encompass all of American life in our vision; and, what is more, the vision can't be limited to our nation. Unless there's a destiny for the planet, there isn't a destiny for any of us. We're going to have to fashion a world in which each group is free to develop its own variations on a universal value system that honors justice, peace, and the worth of each person.

The New out of the Old

We cannot return to the secular traditions we once observed nor to old religions as they once were. There's never a road back. Religious or secular traditions that retain their vitality are always reshaping themselves to express their fundamental spirit in terms that are responsive to the needs and realities of the day. We must play a role in that evolutionary process, building on those portions of existing religious or secular traditions that lend themselves to incorporation into a moral order that will serve the evolving future.

Many contemporary intellectuals will not approach that task with zest. Looking at the world's great religious and moral traditions, they find elements that have no authenticity for today and reject them out of hand. But letting the new evolve out of the old is not really a matter of choice: whether we wish it or not, our visions of the future are selective revisions of our past. Historians chide us for imagining a past "golden age," but it is inevitable. The memories we share are a selection of those times when we were our best selves, or when we were heroic, or when life was serene. We excise the times when we were our worst selves.

Fortunately, our able and disciplined historians save us from a silly and self-deceptive nostalgia. Yet it is almost impossible for us to think hopefully about the future at all except with the aid of idealized memories. Thus for our future we want presidents who resemble the great ones of our past—magnified, retouched, and idealized. Some of the attraction of "citizen participation" involves idealized memories of the town meeting. So it is with all of the attitudes that move humans and human societies: they are attached to memories, legends, symbols, myths, and belief systems of long standing. New elements take root slowly, often over centuries. The sterility of so many of the faddish cults of the day bear testimony to the fact. They lack roots.

Don't mistake me. This is no time for retreat into comfortable doctrines and dreams of the past. All I'm saying is that the "new vision" will not be rootless. It will build on existing traditions that pervade our literature, drama, folk tales, legal forms, and institutional practices—traditions that affect our conscious and un-

conscious minds in innumerable subtle ways. A sense of
the future arising out of that background will resonate
in the deepest chambers of our being.

We need the help not only of leaders, political and
other, but also of artists—poets, novelists, painters,
sculptors, dramatists. And the artists need us to need
them. William Irwin Thompson was right when he said;
"[We] tried to make an entire culture out of Art and
the Artist. But art grows out of culture and is fed by culture. If art has to feed upon itself for mythology, it will
die. . . . "

And Joyce Carol Oates is correct when she says, "Poetry—like all art—demands that its subject be made
sacred. Art is the sacralizing of its subject."

Among the many subjects that art might celebrate
are those men and women who have tried over the
millenniums of recorded history to make the human
enterprise work, those imperfect, irrepressible men
and women who strove to create order out of moral
chaos even in the darkest times; who sought against
great odds to extend the area of justice; the freedom
lovers; the meaning seekers. Let art celebrate the bat-
tered but inviolable dignity of those flawed, durable,
dreaming creatures.

Not One Vision but Many

We should set ourselves the task of creating not just one
new pattern but many new patterns, not just one formulation of the future but many. One need not seek an
overarching vision. Many constructive people will take
the large and small actions that their intuition leads
them to, not waiting until an architectonic vision seizes
them. The visions of the future will spring up in many

places, not identical but with strong common elements. We have already, in earlier chapters, touched on some of those common elements; we shall touch on others in the chapters that follow.

6 || The Springs of Action

When farsighted people see their society headed for trouble, they may seek to arouse the citizenry to action. If the trouble threatens to be catastrophic, they find it hard to understand why the society does not respond heroically. But most societies most of the time are unheroic and quite incapable of commanding their fate. If they are lucky, they ride Fortune's wave (with a conqueror's air); if they are unlucky, they drift somnambulistically into deeper and deeper difficulties.

Historically, populations have sometimes been brought to a high pitch of motivation by disaster (particularly wars), sometimes by a combination of coercion and propaganda (the totalitarian formula), and occasionally by fortunate circumstances that bring a great release of human energies (such as our own westward movement).

A free society concerned to motivate its people, then, faces the question of how to do so without the stimulus of disaster, without resorting to coercion and propaganda, and without awaiting a historical stroke of luck.

Sources of Lowered Motivation

Motivation and morale are relatively low in the United States today, certainly compared with what we have known through most of our history. It is worth speculating on some of the factors involved.

The most obvious is that we're no longer a struggling young society dreaming of its future, no longer lean and hungry, but a big-bellied, mature, "successful" society.

Equally obvious is the element of disillusionment. Many Americans once believed that man and society not only could be perfected but were approaching that goal with lively speed; they have since learned how wrong they were. The capacity of advanced, "civilized" societies to conduct themselves savagely has forced a reevaluation of long-cherished illusions. The willingness of freely elected officials to deceive and defraud the electorate has shaken our confidence. The persistence of social ills in our prosperous nation has cast its shadow.

Still another barrier to high motivation is the widely shared view that our civilization exists to make us "happy" and to spare us problems and pain. Many highly motivated people recognize that their commitment to a goal may lead them into painful, unhappy, even dangerous situations—and are undismayed. Their willingness to take the risk isn't as unnatural as their concerned friends are apt to believe. The human organism, product of millions of years of evolution, was designed for a world in which pain and danger are realities.

None of this should be taken as encouragement to individuals to kill themselves with work, or neglect their families, or engage in behavior that is destructive of other values. My purpose is just to point out that effort in pursuit of goals is a very human and satisfying kind of behavior. (I am not speaking solely of those whom the world describes as "people of action." Some of the liveliest of goals involve scholarship and reflection.) We are problem seekers. Scientists are generally regarded as finders of answers, but they often describe themselves as finders of problems—and it is just that process that keeps science a vital enterprise. When problems don't seem readily available, we invent them. Most games are invented problems, and a great many people fill their so-called leisure with activity indistinguishable from work except that it is self-initiated and uncompensated. Anyone who has pursued a little white ball around a golf course understands the principle. Is it too easy a problem? Put in more sand traps.

The truth is that most human beings are so constructed that they want something active to do, something that tests them, that engages their mind and their will, that involves not only effort but purposefulness. If they are paid for it, it's called work, and they're not supposed to enjoy it—but many do. It's a shocking thought, but there it is.

The work ethic has been in bad odor with some of our emancipated intellectuals. They see it as an Establishment trick for exploitation of workers, or as the enemy of sensual or spiritual ways of life. Neither view does justice to the deep-seatedness of the work ethic, which has cropped up strongly in societies of widely differing religious beliefs. In most cultures there are many men and women who are, by nature, workers, burden shoulderers, problem tacklers—and can't help it any more than they can help breathing or getting hungry. Given that fact, and given the respect that naturally accrues to those who carry more than their share of the day's burden, the emergence of a work ethic is really not a particularly startling social outcome. Quite distinguishable from the work ethic is the view—too widely accepted in our society—that only compensated economic activity (a job) confers acceptable adult status. We should recognize and honor the fact that the human need for purposeful activity can be satisfied in many ways.

I've commented extensively on activity we usually associate with the word "work," but nothing I have said should be taken as denigrating the value of the contemplative life or of those forms of leisure that involve other dimensions of experience—art, nature, companionship, play.

Still another ingredient in today's lowered motivation is the lack of positive views of the future to give us a shared sense of direction and lend tone and tautness to our efforts. We have no dreams of greatness to come. We have lost the old dreams and faiths. We can envisage the anti-Utopias of Orwell and Huxley, but most people simply don't see anything ahead that lifts the spirit. The outlook is bleak for our society unless we can generate a view of the future that is not only credible but that draws upon the deep, moving forces, universal and eternal, that stir mankind to action and belief. We can do it, but not by following the path of recent years.

Even the most sensible proposal for a better future provokes the cynic to say, "I'll believe it when I see it." The tough-minded social activist Saul Alinsky turned the phrase around and said, "We'll see it when we believe it."

What Moves People

High-minded people speaking of the goals we must achieve rarely mention sheer physical energy as an essential ingredient to motivation and morale; but much of our capacity to work toward desirable ends depends on our physical drive and durability. Within the normal range of a healthy population, differences in physical vigor cannot compare with psychological factors as a motivational ingredient. But in dealing with populations that exist in the depths of poverty, one must never forget how malnutrition and disease affect the level of physical energy and hence motivation and morale.

For some people, the assertion that physical vigor is one of the roots of morale in action, even action with lofty intellectual objectives, will appear to detract from the "nobility" of the goals involved. But mind and body are inseparable. That's the way we were designed.

Of equal importance is dedication to beliefs that require action. Much of the lethargy in a decaying social system is traceable to the large number of individuals who no longer believe in what they are doing. They have been left without essential nutritive elements in their psychic diet. Some plod on dully through the routines of life. Others seek diversions desperately, but find themselves in the grip of a boredom that no diversion can relieve.

Those who can find something to believe in and work for are granted a blessed release from emptiness. Thus we see not only the emergence of new movements within established religions but a lively commerce in concocted "faiths" put forward by "spiritual leaders" who are in fact entrepreneurs—shrewd and manipulative vendors of commitment. Those adults who worry that some young people are seeking out such entrepreneurs should ask themselves what is missing in our culture that leads youth on this search.

People steeped in sophistication and world-weariness may make light of faith as an ingredient in human hope and morale. But humans are the only living creatures that worship, that experience reverence, wonder, and awe, that reach out to something beyond themselves. They do not all reach out in the same way, but the reaching out is an historically significant ingredient in human motivation.

The motivation of individuals is positively affected if there is high morale in the group of which they are a part. (Even those who rebel, rebel with zest.) That is why one may expect bad consequences when we begin to believe that our society is no longer capable of solving its problems. Or when people come to believe that what they do in behalf of the group can't possibly "make a difference." Or when large numbers of people feel that they are excluded from the society.

In the same vein, individual morale is deeply affected by group expectations. If the group expects a lot, individuals will be motivated to give accordingly. Studies of courage among infantrymen in World War II showed that the main factor in personal valor was the morale of the unit and the individual's desire not to let the group down.

The teacher's comment, "I expect better of you," is a powerful stimulus to performance. Equally powerful is the negative effect when family, teachers, and others expect the individual to perform badly. One of the melancholy consequences of the oppression of some humans by others is that the oppressed often accept the judgment that they are unworthy—and behave accordingly. When the community regards minority group children as poor educational material, all too often parents and teachers share the community's view, consciously or unconsciously, and the children come to share it too, performing as the community expects them to.

Incentives

Some people contribute importantly to the society without expectation of recompense; but most are moved to greater effort if they anticipate an appropriate reward—and all societies offer such rewards. A totalitarian society seeks to restrict incentives to those conferred by the state—power, status, special privileges, escape from punishment—and it uses those incentives extensively. In a free society, government does not maintain a monopoly on the system of incentives; it assumes that a diversity of incentives is necessary and desirable in a vital society.

Challenge

The longer I live, the more I respect enthusiasm. There is no perfection of technique that will substitute for the lift of spirit that enthusiasm produces. Some people keep their zest until the day they die. They keep a sense of curiosity. They care about things. They reach out. They enjoy. They risk failure. They may even allow themselves some moderately cheerful expectations for the time ahead. Such expectations may be greeted with skepticism in the current climate, but we should welcome the buoyancy from which they spring. Otherwise, in our world-weary wisdom, we shall be unresponsive to challenges that keep societies alive and moving.

Today, the challenges are many and demanding: to find a means of ending wars before we stumble into the final war; to save our planetary environment; to meet basic human needs in a world of resource constraints;

to make real the ideas of justice, liberty, and individual dignity; to redesign modern social organization to balance the claims of the individual and the claims of society; to end the abuse of power; to enable people to believe in themselves and something beyond themselves.

The challenge is there. The task is to open our eyes.

7 || Responsibility

Recently in our society self-exoneration has become a national habit. A friend wrote me not long ago recalling his own attitudes and those of his contemporaries in graduate school a decade ago:

> We were great critics. We complained that our society didn't provide us with adequate spiritual nourishment. We rejected established religions. We criticized the nation's leaders. We expressed contempt for our teachers. We were like children demanding service and then scorning what was served.
>
> We never thought of ourselves as responsible for anything. *They* were responsible—always the unidentified *They*, the invisible ones who ran the society. Our only responsibility was to see through their hypocrisies and complain. It was a great excuse for doing nothing.
>
> I count the beginning of my maturity from the day I began to see the childishness of all that. I decided to accept responsibility for my world—to the limit of reality. Obviously I couldn't accept responsibility for thunderstorms or nationwide depressions. But where I could

64

possibly imagine that a fraction of responsibility lay on me, I resolved to welcome that responsibility.

In authoritarian or strongly traditional societies, responsibilities are rigorously defined, and failure to meet them results in punishment or severe disapproval. As the authority of law and custom has diminished, the idea of responsibility has been harder to sustain. Yet no serious person can accept the currently popular formulas of self-exoneration. One hears people explain their unprincipled behavior by saying, "Everybody's doing it." It's an excuse that is widely used, though not by people with a sense of their own dignity. My integrity is not dependent on my neighbor's integrity: it's my own project.

One hears people excuse their greed or duplicity by asserting that there is no reward for decent behavior; they mean, of course, no material or externally conferred award. But if decent behavior depended on material rewards, it would have died out early in the history of the race. If I behave well, it will satisfy me and bring a favorable verdict from my inner jury, those few respected ones whose judgment is crucial to my self-respect. In stable communities, ethical behavior does sometimes bring material rewards, but those who behave ethically for that reason aren't necessarily virtuous. They are investors in morality.

One hears people excuse failure to do their duty in the community by saying they're powerless. Here we move beyond the vulgar forms of self-exoneration into a range of highly sophisticated excuses. "I'm powerless. . . . The society is fundamentally corrupt. . . . What can I do?" This argument not only gets the speaker off the hook of responsibility; it leaves him looking morally superior—a neat trick.

When people say they are powerless to influence the

values of the day, one is bound to wonder how they made the calculation. One exemplary act may affect millions of lives. Or even one life. I will cling to the idea that what I do is not without effect, and that I am responsible for the consequences.

Each Is Responsible

Each of us is responsible. We must be prepared to learn with humility from those wiser than we, whether our forebears or our contemporaries; but having done so, each of us must know that he or she has to bring those teachings to life.

New conceptions of where we ought to be headed as a nation and as a world will emerge—are already emerging, some would say—from the minds of people, not from that political abstraction, "the people," but from individuals. The material out of which we shall build a new world is not something outside ourselves, to be searched for as Ponce de León sought the Fountain of Youth; it is in us, in our minds, in our character, in our memory of things past, in our hopes for the future. We cannot wait for elected leaders to sketch that future for us. We are the source. We shall conceive it, we shall design it, and we shall put it into operation. We are the builders and the rebuilders. More and more individuals are beginning to understand that concept and to act on it. It is an exhilarating burden for those strong enough to bear it. And more and more individuals are finding that strength within them.

There are real dilemmas facing those who choose today to follow the path of responsibility. Which path is it? Older and more stable societies defined the individual's obligations in detail. People were rarely in doubt as to what was expected of them. Today the authority of law and custom has been greatly diminished, and swift social change has blurred the once-clear lines of duty. Guidance from family, church, school, and community is whispery and contradictory.

Many individuals respond by walking away from the whole idea of responsibility, thus doing their bit to move the society further toward chaos. Others find within themselves both the impulse and the strength to rebuild a disintegrating ethic of responsibility.

But it can never be a wholly individual enterprise. There is a fatal flaw in the notion of totally independent responsibility. The poet's outburst, "I am the master of my fate; I am the captain of my soul" is inspiring but untrue. Excessive glorification of the individual's capacity to be personally "responsible" without supports outside the self invites overweening pride. It assumes an omnipotent individual purpose that doesn't accord with any known reality. All the major world religions— as well as most secular philosophies—have found it necessary to combat the human impulse to glorify individual purpose. If every strong individual constructed a wholly autonomous framework of responsibility, it would bring us to chaos as quickly as any epidemic of irresponsibility.

If the society is disintegrating, the responsibility of the individual is *to join with others* in the tasks of regeneration. The individual is a part of something larger —a community, a cultural and spiritual heritage, humankind.

The Relaxation of Purpose

Unfortunately, nothing is uncomplicated in this world, and if we foster an ethic of individual moral responsibility, we must face up to the pathologies of purpose. Just as excessive individual pride must be tempered by a sense of the larger contexts in which our strivings occur, so a compulsive sense of purpose must be curbed. This is especially true in a society in which religion and traditional ways have lost so much ground. No longer believing in God's will nor in a social order that must not be defied, some people delude themselves that all obstacles will give way if their own sense of purpose is sufficiently firm and unyielding. That path leads to intolerance of opposition, ulcers, and ultimate disillusionment.

It is folk wisdom that strength of purpose can defeat itself. One can become so intent as to disable oneself. Every athlete, every dancer, every musician learns that there are moments when trying too hard is counterproductive. They have learned in practice what the Zen masters teach us: there is a time when one must stop straining and let the performance happen. It would be misleading to say that the performer is now without purpose. What is involved is a wholly different approach to purpose.

In life itself, there is a time to seek inner peace, a time to rid oneself of the tension and anxiety of striving. Indeed, some Asian religious teachers counsel passivity as the only way to wisdom and truth. Lao-Tse said, "Without looking, you shall see; without moving, you shall know; without doing, you shall achieve." Few Westerners can accept that degree of passivity (and indeed few Asians accept it in practice), but the truth remains that relaxation of purpose has its place in life. One of the beauties of Zen is that it deals not just with the tranquillity of inaction, as in meditation, but with the tranquillity possible in action.

Oriental quietism and the element of world-rejection in both Eastern and Western religions are part of the truth, but striving, planning, hoping, and trying are too.

Neither purpose nor passivity is superior; each is a part of the rhythm of life. There is a time to seize and a time to loosen one's grasp, a time for effort and a time for repose. Purpose is a consequence of biological vitality; but purposefulness without limit can destroy. The moment comes when the striving must let up, when wisdom says, "Be quiet."

Perspective on the human condition helps. Some of the more doctrinaire existentialists notwithstanding, I am not wholly free to choose. A large part of what I do is determined by physical and behavioral characteristics developed over millions of years of evolution, by the genetic background of my family, or by impulses so deeply traditional in my culture that I am hardly aware of them. These limitations need not leave me with a sense of fatalism. Perhaps my conscious purposes account for only a fraction of my behavior; but that fraction is the bearer of my sense of moral responsibility.

Both aspects of myself are important—the part that is determined by my background and the part that is mine to shape. Out of the first part, the behavior that links me with my species, my genetic line, my religious or cultural traditions, comes the deep identities that give me a sense of oneness with something larger and makes me feel at home in the universe. That part says to me: "You are living a moment in the drama of human life on this earth. The great themes of birth and death, of love, sorrow, and suffering replay themselves through you. Don't imagine that you are unique, or that your struggles are the turning point in the great train of events. Let the ancient drama go on, and take strength from your time-honored part in it."

But the other part of me, the part that is mine to command, says, "You can play your part well or badly. Play it well."

8 || The Individual and the Group

A few years ago a New York City bus driver, in a burst of personal rebellion, let all his passengers off in the middle of a busy day and headed his empty vehicle for Florida. His employers weren't happy about it; but to the newspaper readers of the nation he was a kind of folk hero. They understood. And their understanding flowed from an underground reservoir of hostility toward all the complex, disciplined functioning of modern social organization, all the schedules, supervisors, rules, and hierarchies. With respect to these targets, inarticulate rebellion seethes in the breast of even the highly conventional individual.

The anger is not capricious. There is a threat to individuality inherent in any large, elaborately organized technological society. Losing confidence in their capacity to have any effect on the events that shape their lives, individuals end up feeling powerless. Inflation, crime, unemployment, international tensions, and other problems of the day seem wholly beyond the reach of individual action. Losing a sense of belonging, a sense of their identity and their relationship to the whole, they end up feeling anonymous. They believe that they have little opportunity to participate. They are driven to conformity. The specialization of contemporary social organization deprives them of versatility; and they find it hard to be whole men and women in a society that fragments their lives, surrounds them with abstractions, and separates them from nature. Relationships are depersonalized, human communications eroded. Added to all these disintegrative forces are the effects of swift social change: loss of all sense of roots, of continuity between the generations, of shared memories.

The Beehive Model

Unless we discover means of remedial action, the worst is yet to come. The end toward which all modern societies, whatever their ideology, appear to be moving is what one might call the beehive model—a society in which as the total system attempts to perfect itself, the individual is steadily dwarfed. Intricate organizational patterns come naturally to advanced technological societies. And sooner or later, pervasive, monolithic organization destroys individual responsibility, unless great effort is made to prevent that outcome. The individual is coerced by the system.

Our deepest values prompt us to protect the individual from all forms of oppression, including this peculiarly modern form. But there are also pragmatic reasons to do so. The vigor of the society is dependent on the vitality and creativity of the individuals who make it up.

No Place to Hide

Long before Paul Gauguin fled to Tahiti, individuals from the Western industrial nations had begun their unending search for some escape from their increasingly complex societies. A friend of mine, one of the restless seekers, migrated some time ago to a remote spot on the globe noted for its picturesque, preindustrial simplicity.

Returning to this country a year or two later, he told me that in the beginning he had often complimented the local people on how authentic and unspoiled they were. It was quite a shock when one of them made it clear to him that the villagers were tired of hearing him say that. They didn't want to be "authentic" as he chose to define the term. They hungered to be "spoiled" by industrial civilization. One of the village elders admitted to my friend that though he scolded the young people for their new ways, everyone knew the past would never be restored. As he put it, "You can't hide from the passing of the days."

My friend might have spared himself the trip and figured that out at home. But no doubt it was more convincing to travel a long way and hear it from a village elder.

Large-scale organization, advanced technology, and the great, complex, interweaving processes of the modern world are here to stay. We live within elaborate frameworks of law and custom: we are affected by worldwide economic forces and resource constraints and caught up in the interdependence of nations.

We can pretend that those realities don't exist, or that they are unworthy of our attention, but most people will be profoundly affected by them throughout their lives. What we pay for food, whether there are enough jobs to go around, whether we have peace or war—all will be influenced by what happens in those vast interdependent systems. How we conduct ourselves as a nation will affect people on the other side of the globe, and decisions made in foreign capitals will affect us. In 1973 the oil embargo imposed by foreign oil-producing nations seriously destabilized our economy. In the event of a major nuclear war, radioactive fallout will drift into the far hills and valleys where the communes of the counterculture have sought escape from the big world. There's no place to hide.

Human Potentialities

If we accept the realities of modern, large-scale organization, what becomes of individuality? The subject is a difficult one to discuss because one has to talk about the fulfillment of the individual as an individual, and then about the individual as an inescapably social creature. Let's begin with the individual as individual.

It is one of the ironies of human society that individual human beings, acting together, build great institutional structures—governments, churches, corporations—that then tend to devalue individual human beings. But in the sweep of history the institutional structures are as ephemeral as wisps of fog in the breeze of morning. In Spain they say, "Todo decae sino la raza." (Everything decays but the people.) It is true of every society. The primal source of energy, of creativity, of renewal is people. A society concerned for its own continued vitality will be interested in the growth and fulfillment of individual human beings— the release of human potentialities.

The first requirement is that there be equal opportunity and a free flow of talent from all segments of the society into the roles that are crucial to the society's future vitality and growth. Mobility must not be obstructed by artificial barriers of caste or class, wealth or family, race or religion. Quite aside from the moral argument for opportunity, no modern nation can afford to lose the human talent that is so often buried under layers of economic and class discrimination. Modern societies run on talent, yet it's doubtful that any society has ever used more than a fraction of the talent available to it. The rest is blocked by poverty, ignorance, class barriers, prejudice, physical and mental ill health, and so on.

The society must address itself to the removal of the obstacles to growth and fulfillment, whether they stem from imperfections in the society (economic deprivation, race prejudice), in the educational system (poor teaching, inadequate schools), or in the individual (sensory handicaps, mental retardation, emotional disorders).

We know the extraordinary difficulty of achieving even modest progress on those fronts. But those are the directions in which we must strive.

The Individual in Society

So far, so good. But respect for each individual's uniqueness and value must be supplemented by a recognition that humans are social beings. Set aside fantasies of complete individual freedom. Unqualified individualism is an absurdity. We move toward the freedom available to humans only when we recognize that we are not wholly free. We live with the biological potentialities and limitation of a species that has not changed greatly in 50,000 years. We live in a cultural context, some of the roots of which run back 10,000 years. We are, in part, prisoners of our personal history. We are caught in the play of social forces.

When we understand those realities, whether the terms of our understanding are religious or philosophical, when we admit that we are part of something larger, then the only freedom that is possible for humankind opens up to us. Recognition of one's part in a larger drama may lead some individuals to various forms of passivity. But many admirable people have continued to play their role to the hilt, knowing they were not the authors of the great drama in which they act, but acting nonetheless with courage and a sense of purpose.

The community must protect our individuality; in turn, we are the only ones who can shape communities that will ensure that result. We must criticize the community yet nurture it. The tension between individual and group is healthy, but the deepest threat to the integrity of any community is the incapacity of citizens to lend themselves to any worthy common purpose. Individualism that degenerates into anarchism, self-indulgence, or dog-eat-dog exploitation of others is individualism gone wrong. The end to be sought is developed, creative individuals who expend their talents in the service of shared values.

The following chapter will examine more fully the family and community context within which individuality must be preserved.

9 || Family and Community

In a recent television drama, a homeless young drifter living the street life said, "This old society has fallen completely apart. I'm on my own. So are you. So are we all." In a sense he was right, although our society has never been more highly organized. The "falling apart" that he sensed is a disintegration of the stable patterns of relationship that bind one human to others at the level of emotion, loyalty, and meaning.

At the same time that our culture is placing extraordinary pressures on the individual, the tumultuous pace of change is depriving us of all the ancient retreats from personal strain—strong family ties, a closely knit community, secure beliefs, confidence in the continuity of things, a feeling for the past. All those things, in diffuse but effective ways, once lightened the burden the individual had to bear.

The Decay of Community

But we cannot resurrect a world that has disappeared. For several centuries now the trend of history has been toward the disintegration of long-established and cohesive human traditions, institutions, and groups. The revolutions in transportation and communication had a devastating effect on isolated and parochial communities that had nursed their unique beliefs and traits down the centuries. The Scientific and Industrial Revolutions and the torrential change of the past century have left many a thoughtful observer with a sense of inevitable chaos to come.

But chaos is not coming and isn't the problem. The problem is not that patterns of organization will disappear, but that they will take forms wholly inappropriate to deeply rooted human social needs. In earlier times, the ways people interacted were determined by ancient social patterns of the community in which they lived. However unenlightened, by modern standards, those patterns may have been, they generally filled human needs for identity, a sense of belonging, roots, family continuity, and person-to-person allegiance. Today, increasingly, patterns of human interaction are determined by the impersonal dynamics of large-scale organization, by the unintended consequences of technological advance, or by commercially motivated decisions. Whether they also meet human social needs is often a matter of the sheerest chance. A neighbor says, "I don't know anyone here. My company transferred me, and here I am." An old friend writes, "When the new freeway from the city was built, the old village was buried under a huge new suburb. An avalanche couldn't have obliterated it more completely."

It is increasingly difficult in the contemporary world to find those coherent social contexts that we call communities—human groupings that individuals can give allegiance to and that they can accept as defining, in part, who they are. Daniel Bell writes that one's sense of identity is "confirmation by significant others" and points out that community rituals confirm that identity. But the confirming is impossible if the community and "significant others" do not exist. The consequences are far-reaching. It is extremely difficult to preserve the idea of social responsibility within agglomerations of people who have lost a sense of community.

Are we dealing here with a disintegration so fundamental to social functioning that it strikes at the very root of our regenerative capacity? The answer is no: here too regeneration is not only possible but demonstrable. From the dawn of history, the social groupings of family, community, tribe, and village have been shattered over and over—by natural disasters, by wars, by migrations, by plagues. Humans pick themselves up, salvage what they can, and set about the creation of new groupings.

Necessarily, historians have concentrated (until recently) on larger and more formal institutions—the nation-states, organized religions, and economic systems that have provided the chief framework for the life of societies. This emphasis obscures the abundant smaller groups that have been a part of human history from the beginning—kinship groups (family, tribe, clan), hunting and food-gathering bands, and, later, religious sects, guilds, and so on. Focusing on these groups, one is bound to be impressed with the extravagant fertility of humankind in the continuous creation and re-creation of such associations. Humans have freely and creatively formed groups to meet just about any mutual need one might conceive.

The Family

There are social needs that can be met only by small groups in which the indivdual enjoys membership either by birth or long association: kinship groups and groups beyond kinship such as village, neighborhood, church, ethnic enclave, and the like. Such groups tend to provide the individual with roots and identity; a sense of belonging; a role and an opportunity for participation; role models drawn from other members of the group; mutual aid; and shared attitudes that supply a structure of meaning.

Perhaps because the family has met these needs, it is, as Urie Bronfenbrenner has pointed out, "the only social institution that is present in every single village, tribe, people or nation-state . . . throughout history." But today many people are worried about the integrity of the family—not just its integrity but its very survival. One can understand the concern—given the swift changes that have occurred in recent decades. The divorce rate has increased 700 percent since 1900 and has doubled in the past decade; nearly 40 percent of all marriages now end in divorce. In twenty-five years the number of one-parent homes has almost doubled, and the rate of births to unmarried mothers has more than doubled. We now have about 2 million cases of child abuse each year, 200,000 resulting in death. The suicide rate for youths from 15 to 19 years of age has almost tripled in the past twenty years; suicide is now the third leading cause of death among young American whites.

Historians are correct in pointing out that anxieties over the demise of the family have been with us for a long time, and that the family has in fact proven enormously resilient. The function of the family and the patterns of family life have changed more or less continuously over the centuries and are changing now. Even so, recent trends give one pause. The family is one major arena in which we may ensure the regeneration of values.

But the findings of history and anthropology make it clear that there is not one ideal model to which the family must adhere.

The best thing we can do for the family is to provide a social context in which families can survive. The family has been eroded by social forces outside itself; to halt that erosion, society as a whole must act. For example, poverty—particularly in contemporary urban settings—is a proven disintegrator of family life. A full-employment policy, a job guarantee for heads of households, and a rational system of income supports to replace our present badly designed "welfare" system would move us in the right direction. Arrangements permitting the single parent to work and care for children at the same time are urgently needed: flexible work hours, part-time work, child-care programs, and so on. The treatment of families and children in the courts should be redesigned to place far more emphasis on keeping families together.

These are only examples. The family, like the individual, exists in a social context. If that context is disintegrative rather than supportive, the family cannot survive.

New Forms of Community

It is possible that the best thing we can do for the family is to create (or re-create) the kinds of community in which it may flourish. The old-style coherent community provided the family with forms of support that in most places no longer exist. We must invent new support structures. A considerable variety of ideas is now being discussed and tested. For example, the capacity of the family to hold together in the urban context may be considerably enhanced by housing developers who make provision for child-care centers in living units and outpatient arrangements for the elderly who want to live near (but not with) their young people.

This is not to suggest that it will be easy to re-create coherent communities within which individuals will have the opportunity to serve, to be needed, to connect. There isn't any one magic way to restore the idea or the reality of community in this incoherent world. There are numerous possible paths of exploration.

In many contexts it may be possible to preserve or create geographically coherent human settlements in the old patterns. The vast organizational networks of contemporary life will not disappear, but we can create smaller communities within the larger framework. The prospect is not hopeless. We have rediscovered the virtues of smallness. While some small towns are disintegrating, others have found a new vitality and are attracting newcomers who want to escape from the urban environment. Some of the old, distinctive urban neighborhoods are now being consciously protected from disintegrative forces. There is a wide range of experimentation with new forms of community.

Industry and labor can do much to alter patterns of work to provide a greater sense of community and personal involvement on the job, and such experiments are in progress. The workplace has always been underrated as a social environment. It supplies, in adult years, a very high proportion of the individual's social interaction; and the interaction is given coherence and meaning by the binding force of tasks that must be performed collaboratively. It provides another dimension of identity. In urban settings where home and work are separated, it provides an alternative culture in which new roles and self-images develop.

Architects, housing authorities, and real estate developers can help greatly to provide living arrangements that will revive a sense of community. Some—too few —are working at this imaginatively.

The geographically coherent community, with its sense of place and its opportunities for daily interaction; will always be attractive; but there may be a livelier future for geographically dispersed communities. This is not as unfamiliar a concept as it sounds. Historically there have been a great many religious and lay orders that were, in fact, geographically dispersed communities. Some professional, scholarly, and scientific associations today are fairly closely knit communities without geographical definition.

Voluntary Associations

Another form of grouping that may serve some of the significant functions of a community is the voluntary association. This enormously broad category comprises diverse groupings. The legendary capacity of our country to create voluntary groups in profusion has not flagged. In addition to the long-established associations, such as service clubs, social clubs, recreational or hobby clubs, and groups built on common economic interests (unions, trade associations), less traditional organizations are sprouting up. Indeed, one gets the impression that the sheer strength of the disintegrative forces today may have brought—by way of reaction—an exceptional surge in the creation of new groupings.

Consider, for example, the extraordinary proliferation of citizen-action groups, concerned with the environment, consumer affairs, political reform, and many other issues. Their function is generally to forge a participatory link to the larger political community.

In the field of health care, we have seen an astonishing flowering of so-called self-help groups, from the long-established Alcoholics Anonymous to Synanon, clubs for stroke victims, clubs for those who have undergone mastectomy, and so on ad infinitum. Typically such a group is made up of persons who share a powerful binding experience. The group provides not only a sense of belonging but also the opportunity to act on a commonly accepted agenda in the service of deeply shared concerns. Within the context of mutual aid implicit in the very existence of the group, there is generally a strong ethic of individual responsibility.

There is a wave of new religious groups, some arising within the bosom of our own traditional churches, others springing (or purporting to spring) from various Asian religions, and still others wholly novel.

There is the much-publicized emergence of new types of familylike or communitylike living groups, some based on religion, some on ideology, and some describable only as products of the ferment of the 1960s.

Finally, we see groups experimenting with one or another kind of psychological experience or interaction —meditation, communication, reduction of interpersonal barriers, and so on. These groups have suffered from faddishness and commercial exploitation, but anyone who examines them seriously will learn something about the unfilled needs of the individual in today's world.

No one can predict what the kinship and community groupings of the future will look like. But we must hope and expect that they will survive in some form. They contain the answer to the question of how we may preserve individuality, identity, and personal significance in a world of massive corporate and governmental bureaucracies, a world that places enormous distance between individuals and the realities that govern their lives.

10 || Options Unlimited

Limitless Freedom

In the prosperous segments of most Western industrial societies, the ancient limits on human choice are vanishing. Thanks to affluence, technology, and the breakdown of old constraining forces—stable communities, traditional belief systems, customs, and obligations—the scope of individual choice has broadened enormously. And reigning ideologies of individual freedom and enlightened childrearing tend to forbid any narrowing of that scope.

The extraordinary freedom of choice for favored groups today no doubt exacerbates social tensions, since in most of the affluent societies disadvantaged minorities remain who cannot hope to enjoy such choice.

For the affluent, the possibilities are unprecedented. You are free to choose your profession, choose the part of the country (or world) in which you will live, choose your neighbors, your friends, your politics, your reli-

85

gion, your way of speaking, your manner of dress, even your hair color and profile.

But it turns out there are limits beyond which increased choices do not yield an increase in sense of well-being. Limitless freedom isn't as blissful as it might seem. With all the extraordinary opening up of choices, people in general don't seem to be happier—and among those who have the maximum range of choice, many are downright miserable. One is bound to ask whether there is something in human beings that is not well-fitted to a world of limitless options; whether the existence of constraints—even modest constraints, in one or another form—is essential to developing the bony structure of adult character. Could it be that human beings flourish under the reasonable constraints of custom and commonly accepted values?

What kind and amount of "freedom" best suit the needs of mankind is a complicated question. In a society of equals, unlimited freedom for each is out of the question. Your freedom to commit mayhem could interfere with my freedom to remain all in one piece. We begin to grasp what Cicero meant when he said, "We are in bondage to the law in order that we may be free." Without laws, chaos reigns; no one is free.

Generally accepted contemporary opinion does not reflect the complexity of the idea of freedom. The most liberated contemporary thinking still clings to the notion that we will all be better and better as choices expand, as constraints vanish, and as individuals are utterly free to act on whatever impulse moves them. A friend of mine who favors swing-of-the-pendulum theories assures me that this kind of thinking is self-corrective—that as we approach the Day of Overthrow of the Last Inhibition there will come into being, inevitably, a Movement for Reinstatement of Useful Inhibitions.

But I'm not talking about anything so narrow as inhibition versus indulgence. I'm talking about the whole universe of choices that individuals face today—educational, occupational, geographic, conjugal, spiritual, and so on.

Why are we reluctant to face up to the dilemmas inherent in the idea of freedom? Probably because we are acutely aware of historical limitations on choice that have thwarted human fulfillment—limitations that result from poverty and ignorance, from rigidly imposed social doctrines, from political tyranny, from social stratification. Because we reject past limitations so vigorously, we tend to see any hint of a limit on freedom as a move back toward the political subjugation, economic exploitation, or hidebound morality we fought to escape. We want none of that.

We are less alert to the hazards of limitless choice. That is hardly surprising: we have had 10,000 years to learn the consequences of human bondage, and no more than a century to sense the problems of limitless choice. But the casualties are there for all to see. There is the escape from freedom described by Fromm—retreat to a totalitarian context in which one is spared the problem of choice. There is the considerable rate of breakdown, alcoholism, and drug addiction among those who "have everything." (Why are we perpetually astonished to rediscover that people who appear to have everything don't have everything?) And most tragic because least visible, there is the large number of people who simply lose their way and live on confused and defeated. If one feels any compassion at all for such individuals—and how can one not?—some searching questions must be asked.

Isn't it possible that what we need now is not limitless options but a reasonable range of choices within a framework of constraints freely agreed upon—constraints that reflect moral, intellectual, aesthetic, and political perceptions and values? One would hope that we are sufficiently mature in our thinking about freedom to move toward some reasonable discipline of shared values (knowing that we're the last people on earth who would want an imprisoning consensus). One would hope that we might formulate some measure of shared principle and purpose (knowing that it must always be subject to revision). Any such movement back from the swamp of limitless options implies discipline, but a self-imposed discipline that enriches our common life and at the same time provides the opportunities for the free exploration of alternatives so essential to human growth.

One kind of voluntary constraint is to be seen in the commitments made by individuals to something beyond the self—commitments to a set of standards or to some conception of a moral order; to religion; to loved ones; to one's fellow humans. Only if they have made such commitments can men and women find meaning in their lives and achieve full moral stature. Some people equate "commitment" with certain lines of work—teaching, nursing, the ministry—and think of those occupations as somehow opening the way to a personal nobility greater than is possible to, say, a steelworker or an umbrella salesman. But such a distinction is impossible to accept. Doing any legitimate job excellently in itself reflects an admirable kind of commitment. Moreover, commitment to values beyond the self has no necessary relation to one's line of work. Some people exhibit their deepest commitments quite outside their jobs: in their family relationships, in their friendships, in their religious life, in the way they treat their fellow beings, in the goals and standards they set for themselves. There are people who make the world better just by being the kind of people they are. It really matters very little whether they are behind the wheel of a truck, or bringing up a family, or running a business.

The Edgeless Ego

One consequence of limitless options is that for the large segment of the population economically above the poverty level in our own society, few impediments remain to vaulting aspirations and limitless expectations of new experience. All the glittering promises of the modern world have diminished our sense of man's limitations. Somehow the idea has gotten around that there are virtually no limits to the possibilities for human achievement and joy, even ecstasy, provided we're sufficiently enlightened.

All of this has turned out to be, for many people, a devastating trap. Every child can't grow up to be a brain surgeon or a novelist. Every adult can't be an ecstatic human being. All too many people today are trapped between society's assurances of limitless achievement and the real limits set by their own potentialities or by circumstance. Some accept society's assurances and flog themselves down the road to inevitable failure. Others give up altogether. The lucky—or sensible—ones arrive at some workable accommodation between their aspirations and what is possible.

Fortunately, many people achieve such an accommodation. But for others under the lure of limitless possibilities, the ego expands pathologically. It no longer recognizes boundaries. It accepts what it takes to be the assertion of our culture that there are no limits to what you can do or experience. You can win the world's adoring regard, perform legendary deeds, be anything, do anything. The consequence for some is an insatiability, a Faustian hunger for experience that leaves the individual haggard in spirit if not in visage.

It is interesting that in the circles where expanded egos congregate, there is much talk of liberation from sexual, familial, political, and religious constraints in the name of the free intellect, the free senses, the free spirit. But no one mentions the force that most often rages for total freedom: the insatiable ego. Every constraint becomes an affront. Why have I not achieved great things? Why have my great potentialities not made themselves felt? Why have all the experiences not fulfilled me? Have I missed something? There must be more. Must I travel still further, acquire more material possessions, find still other sexual partners, seek newer forms of therapy?

In such an atmosphere, it's hardly surprising that we encounter individuals who nurse a deep grievance: life owes them something—if only some kind of recognition—and has not yet delivered. And it may explain in part, as other observers have pointed out, instances of apparently ordinary individuals, loners as a rule, who burst out of obscurity to perform some spectacular act (stand on a skyscraper ledge, point a gun at a president).

We are not very good at communicating to our children that life has always been hard and always will be, that the world was not designed for our personal enjoyment.

Human Relationships

We have seen a fading of the old-fashioned notion that the basic relationships of one's life—friends, lovers, family, work associates—will probably endure. And there seems to be little or no mourning for the passing of the old-style relationships, with their formalities and their durability. Their requirements of loyalty and commitment appear oppressive to many contemporary Americans.

Some writers celebrate a wholly new approach to relationships. The authentic relationship, they say, is between two people who fulfill each other in some way at that moment (half a year, half a day, half an hour). No formalities, no commitments, no strings, no past, no future. Enjoy the connection while it's enjoyable, and then end it. Two atoms collide, and then each moves on to new collisions. No adversity, no challenge to emotional wisdom, no bitterly acquired knowledge of one's own failings, no hard-won understanding of another human's special mixture of flaws and strengths, no enduring. Just collisions of convenience.

Relationships, in the new doctrine, aren't something you are born to or grow up with. You set out to find them—or manufacture them. Then they are your own. And as with other modern fabrications, the period of manufacture is not expected to take long: instant friendship. And like many other manufactured goods, the product must be disposable when no longer useful. When you are bored with what you have, get rid of it.

But anyone who has watched the random collisions can see that something is missing. No one who has the slightest compassion for those involved can fail to detect the lack of fulfillment beneath the surface. Could it be that most humans are not in fact ideally suited for random collisions? Could it be that most of us need at least a few settled and structured relationships? Could it be that the failure to make such commitments ensures perpetual adolescence—and, beneath all the surface activity, loneliness?

Formality in Relationships

When the twentieth century began, there were still rules and customs governing the relationships between man and wife, young men and women, parents and children, laymen and clergy, worker and employer, student and teacher, host and guest, old and young. Each had his or her socially prescribed duties in the relationship. Tradition determined the terms of address to be used, the permissible degree of informality, and the tone and style of any encounter.

By the middle of the century—at least in the United States—most of that was gone. The whole idea of formalized relationships had almost vanished, as had the idea that one's role in a relationship entailed certain obligations.

Yet the most casual observation of human behavior reveals that *some* degree of formality may enrich and strengthen human relationships. Each person may play his or her own role in such a relationship with dignity, even though each plays a different role. It does not diminish the dignity of a student to accord a measure of respect to his teacher. Nor is casualness the ultimate evidence of sincerity and genuineness in human interaction. All formality is not *mere* formality. And the current notion that authentic feeling should always triumph over outward forms is nonsense. There are emotions so destructive or exploitative that they must be held within bounds if social living is to be possible.

Myth and Reality

In some measure what we are seeing is a justified reaction to the romanticized, prettied-up images of love, friendship, and family relations that prevailed in some societies prior to the mid-twentieth century. Many who believed the prettied-up myths were bitterly disappointed to find them false. Why not face the bedrock fact that human relationships—between parents and children, man and woman, friend and friend—are flawed, as human nature is flawed? Even successful marriages involve conflict, pain, and unresolved differences: even the deepest friendships involve failures of understanding, periods of disaffection, and mixed judgments of one another. Hardly any human relationship is free of hidden resentments (never resolved because they are never aired) that accumulate and sometimes explode. And of course there are excellent reasons for ending some relationships.

In the ties that are a part of one's life history—parents, family and childhood friends—the flaws are apt to be particularly apparent. But they are the flaws of all human ties. The relationships are imperfect because we are imperfect. Casual, here-today-gone-tomorrow relationships are not more perfect; they simply enable us to avoid one aspect of reality. And in fleeing that aspect of reality we find ourselves in the empty, lonely world of throwaway relationships. Deep and durable relationships do not constitute the whole of life, but most people need them, and some need them desperately.

11 || Citizens and Their Government

Ask parents about the schools, and they complain vehemently. Ask about taxes, and the response is apt to be stormy. Inflation, utility rates, crime—all evoke vigorous comment. Then mention "citizenship," and everyone yawns. Somehow all those burning issues and the idea of citizenship don't connect.

The Downward Spiral

Too many citizens today feel they are cut off from the decision centers of their own society. Somewhere in the vast bureaucracies, public and private, an action is taken that affects their lives; but they can't know who made the decision, or why, or how. They can't exercise the familiar prerogative of complaining to the manager because they don't know how to find him. And they suspect that if they did find him he would turn out to be a computer.

There are large numbers of citizens who no longer

feel that the society is their venture. They don't know whose it is, but they are sure it isn't theirs. It is hardly surprising, then, that large numbers of people have, in the phrase of the 1960s, "dropped out." The young people who take to the road and join the enclaves of the counterculture are only a fraction of the dropouts. Throughout the ranks of conventional citizens, there are many who have lost all sense of connection with their own society. They are stay-at-home exiles.

This estrangement has curious consequences for politics. Feeling powerless, people have little impulse to channel their frustrations into constructive political action. They are resentful but inactive, hostile but inert. They are angry, but they won't vote.

Unfortunately, as citizens grow passive, it becomes ever more inviting for unscrupulous leaders to abuse the power entrusted to them, to obtain the consent of the governed by fraudulent means, to deceive the public "for the public's good." (Hitler once wrote, "You cannot believe how much you have to deceive a nation in order to govern it.")

In a downward spiral, disillusioned citizens grow politically inert, and leaders are tempted to exploit that inertness in ways that bring deeper citizen disillusionment. Down and down it goes. To reverse the spiral, those citizens who are not wholly disillusioned must work to make our instruments of self-government worthy of respect, which in turn may lead to the restoring of confidence.

Participation

Active citizen participation is not only good democratic doctrine; it is essential to renewal. Institutions are forever decaying; individuals regenerate the society.

Of course, many people will have worthy commitments in directions other than citizenship (job, family, church, school), and they may be doing just as much to strengthen the society as those who are more politically active. Such people will fulfill their citizen duties by living within the law, instructing their children in the obligations of citizenship, voting, and following public affairs intelligently.

But others will choose to do more. Only a fraction will be community leaders or brave critics, but that fraction is enough. The important thing is to keep the society sufficiently open so that the active fraction can come from any segment.

Citizen participation may take many forms—voting, campaign activities, testifying at hearings, sitting on citizen boards, participating in citizen watchdog organizations, and so on. But the strengthening of citizen participation also requires effort in other dimensions. It means giving full rights of citizenship and personhood to all who have been denied those rights. It means breathing new life into the constitutional guarantees of individual freedom and working to preserve the rule of law.

And participation can be understood to involve broader and deeper matters than the conventional political process. In a society at its healthiest, a substantial portion of the populace feels that as individuals they are a part of something important that is happening. If we may judge by historical examples, such a feeling is not necessarily a conscious judgment; it may be a wordless, intuitive sense of unfolding possibilities. In our first century following the Declaration of Independence, men and women who were wholly out of touch with political events often experienced an exhilarating sense of being part of something—of a new and growing nation, an adventure, a moment in history.

When individuals have little or no confidence that they are participating in a significant or worthy venture, the vitality of the society is impaired.

Open and Accountable Government

It is redundant to say that in a self-governing nation citizens should be able to call their leaders to account. What else would self-government be? Yet, in an imperfect world, we must constantly remind ourselves of the requirement of accountability.

Crucial to accountability is open government. Indeed, openness ranks second only to the rule of law as a necessary ingredient of self-government. Through control of the media, or through secrecy, those in power may deny citizens the information they need in order to hold government accountable. The older forms of tyranny denied citizens, without pretense, any opportunity to participate in their own government. Some of the new tyrannies involve more subtle strategies: citizens are urged to participate, but the propaganda machine tells them what to do, and the information reaching them is manipulated so that they are denied an independent base of judgment.

In practical terms, open government requires freedom of the press, disclosure of lobbying activities and sources of campaign funds, open meetings, freedom-of-information statutes, and financial disclosure by high officials. There are necessary limits on openness in matters that involve invasions of personal privacy, national security, the administration of justice, and certain international negotiations. But past governmental practice has involved secrecy far beyond any rational need. We are now changing that.

The Instruments of Self-Government

Some of our Founding Fathers liked the saying, "Eternal vigilance is the price of liberty." But our 200-year history tells us that free people are not eternally vigilant. They keep dozing off; and meanwhile their liberties are eroded. Generally, before it's too late, they wake up and combat the threat to their liberties. But if successful, they are all too likely to doze off again. So wise citizens will make the most of the moments of wakefulness to ascertain that our institutions for ensuring accountability—the courts, the media, Congress, citizen organizations—are in fact sleepless monitors of our liberties.

The prime instrument of accountability, the electoral process, must be protected with jealous concern. That means detailed attention to voter-registration problems, an open nominating process, the integrity of elections, getting out the vote, and statutes prohibiting subversion of campaigns through espionage and sabotage. These may seem technical matters, but most of the processes on which life and society depend, from cell metabolism to the system of justice, are technical.

The whole web of government, at all levels from city hall to the White House, offers opportunities for citizen involvement. In the 1960s, the slogan "citizen participation" connoted mainly small meetings in which citizens earnestly expressed their views. But no matter how sound the consensus, if there was one, the result rarely went beyond *that* meeting *that* evening. The tens of thousands of citizen groups meeting around the country weren't connected to any central nervous system to ensure that their views were communicated to the decision-making centers of the society.

Yet there existed, and had existed for two centuries, a governmental network that the Founding Fathers had originally supposed would be an instrument for citizen participation. That long-established system—local, state, and federal—wasn't working, which is precisely why aroused citizens were groping for new ways of communicating their concerns.

It's no secret what was wrong with the old networks of government—city hall, county boards of supervisors, state legislatures, Congress, the federal agencies. Some parts were paralyzed by their own mediocrity. Some parts had been bought up lock, stock, and barrel by moneyed interests. Some parts were wholly anachronistic and would have to be redesigned to serve contemporary purposes.

Not surprisingly, it occurred to some citizens that perhaps their most effective contribution to citizen participation would be to repair that venerable and decayed system. Thus the whole movement toward openness and accountability in government that arose in the 1970s was in a sense a redirection of the citizen-participation movement of the 1960s.

The War of the Parts against the Whole

Citizens should give at least part of their attention to the public interest as they understand it—recognizing that others may understand it differently—the interest of the total community, state, nation, or planet. This is not to say that they should ignore self-interest: our polity expects and requires individuals and groups to speak out vigorously on their own particular concerns. But the voices of special interest groups are on the whole well represented in the national chorus. There are rarely enough individuals speaking out for what they conceive to be the public interest.

Citizens must not, of course, make the naïve assumption that having identified what they believe to be the public interest, all they need do is hand the problem over to the federal government, appropriate a lot of money, and consider the problem solved. Sometimes the public interest is best served by turning to the federal government; sometimes not. And when citizens do turn to government, they must hold it closely accountable for what it does.

In the society as a whole, organized special interests —business, labor, farmers, the professions—introduce massive rigidities into the social process. There is nothing inherently wrong in the competition of special interests; it is well within the tradition of pluralistic societies. But sometimes powerful interests gain such a grip on the political process that ordinary citizens haven't a chance of being heard or exerting influence.

At other times the interests bringing pressure on the political process are so numerous and tenacious that they paralyze the society's problem-solving capacity. To comprehend this paralysis as the policy maker experiences it, imagine a checker player confronted first by a bystander who puts a thumb on one checker, saying, "Go ahead and win; just don't touch this checker," and then by another bystander who puts a thumb on another checker, saying, "Don't touch this one," and then another bystander and another . . . Given enough such spectator-participants, soon there are only thumbs, no moves. Ironically, the owners of the thumbs —the special interests—don't want to make the game unwinnable; they just want to ensure that their particular checker will be untouched. How many times have we seen a major American city helpless in the face of grave municipal problems, while every possible solution is blocked by one or another powerful union, commercial interest, or political element. Each has achieved veto power over a piece of any possible solution, and no one has the power to solve the problem. Thus in an oddly self-destructive conflict, the parts wage war against the whole. Far from being a minor political dilemma, this is the central problem of pluralism today, and one of the emerging problems of an increasingly interdependent world.

Loving but Critical Attention

Politics and government, like all other parts of the society, need the loving but critical attention of citizens. Every parent knows how those attitudes intermingle in the nurture of a child. We don't normally think of society as requiring our parental nurture, but it does. We shape and reshape it. Without our caring hands it would quickly die.

Criticism is in plentiful supply today, but for many intelligent Americans the word "loving" as applied to one's attitude toward society is a little embarrassing. It's time to dispel that shadow of embarrassment.

It's not hard to see why the shadow was cast. There is an unattractive kind of group allegiance that is an extension of egotism, that rules out criticism, breeds arrogance, assumes superiority of one's own kind over others, and sanctions inhumane behavior toward others. The wars that have plagued humankind have all too often been associated with that kind of bigoted allegiance. It has given patriotism a bad name—and that's a pity. In an interdependent world, a world capable of self-destruction, one must acknowledge broad allegiances—to humankind, to the planet—but this doesn't require the rejection of love of country, any more than love of country requires us to reject love of family.

For my part, I am skeptical of those who profess their love for humankind but can't bring themselves to love that particular portion of humankind that populates their own country. I am skeptical of those Americans who can't bring themselves to love their country because there are injustices in the American past. There are injustices in the history of any society. People who reject their own heritage and tradition on such grounds are creating a fatal separation between themselves and their kind. There isn't any way of being humane without accepting human fallibility as a part of one's heritage. To set oneself above and apart from our common heritage is an act of arrogance.

Some of the hostility that our citizens feel toward the federal government today is due to our expecting so much from it. Once people attributed their frustrations to Nature, God, Fate, the ancient order of things, or an immutable social structure. Today we place all our hopes on the way our society is run. We impose on society a heavier burden of expectation than human institutions can possibly carry—and then we make it the target of our scorn and contempt when it fails to meet those exalted expectations.

It doesn't require a psychiatrist to identify the immaturity of that pattern. It would be a maturing act for us to lift some of that burden of childlike expectation and place it back where it belongs—on ourselves. If we are better citizens, we shall have a better government: not a repository for immature expectations, but an instrument for responsible adults who intend to hold that instrument accountable.

12 || The Old Man of Quivira

All too often in the name of patriotism, or religion, or brotherhood, humans have created belief systems and loyalties that are destructive of humane values. How can that be? It is not a question to be answered in a sentence or a paragraph. It is a story of rational belief versus zealotry, of escape from individual moral responsibility, of exclusivity and the invention of enemies, of conspiracy theories, of the uses of organized power.

In the hope of sparing the reader long, dull chapters covering these topics, I have created a fable that distills as many of the complexities as can be managed. I have set the fable in a mythical time and place in order to separate it from any particular present-day context. But every issue dealt with is totally contemporary, easily observable in the world today.

In the city of Quivira, a group of citizens began to meet regularly to study the problems of their community and to explore the need for a philosophy of personal responsibility. Although they ranged in age from eighteen to eighty, they chose to refer to themselves as the Students. They studied the schools, the courts, and other aspects of the society that stirred their curiosity.

At one point they decided to give attention to an individual who was known throughout the region as the Old Man of Quivira. He was believed by some to be a seer, and by others to be a mountebank. The afflicted came to him in large numbers. Tribal leaders came from distant regions to consult with him. He held weekly gatherings, and there was always a crowd.

At the first meeting attended by the Students, a delegation from the River People appeared before the Old Man. They said, "Old Man, our tribe is in trouble. Our customs are no longer honored. There is no loyalty. Families do not hold together. We are no longer strong in war. Vice is triumphant. How can we save ourselves?"

The Old Man meditated for a while and then said, "If you follow my instructions to the letter, I will save you."

"We are ready," said the River People.

"Then you must begin," said the Old Man, "with a compelling set of beliefs. Write down what you believe. If you don't know what you believe, write down what your fathers believed. Then you must require that every member of the tribe subscribe to those beliefs. Totally. No dissent. Tell your people that when they accept these beliefs, they will have surrendered themselves to the central current of history, the path of moral evolution, the pulse of the universe. They will be released from the dull pain of their days and will find peace and a great exhilaration. No more doubt and fear. The energies of the universe will flow through them. Tell them that."

"Are you certain that will help?" asked one of the River People.

"The doctrine will be a safe harbor for the weak and the unstable," the Old Man replied. "It will speak to those whose deepest impulses are toward passionate conviction. Individuals are not strong enough to carry the weight of intellectual and moral responsibility, and this will relieve them of the burden."

The Old Man must have sensed that the Students in his audience were shocked. "Is there disagreement?" he asked, waving a hand toward them. "Speak up!"

His tone was threatening and did not really invite discussion, but one of them spoke.

"We don't believe people should be relieved of the burden of individual moral responsibility, including responsibility to seek the truth without escape into dogma, knowing that fallible humans will never know the final truth."

But the River People were impressed with the Old Man's advice and departed satisfied.

A month later they reappeared. They had written down all of their traditional tribal beliefs, even the ones that were not much honored anymore. "This is our doctrine," they said. The Old Man read it and nodded approvingly.

"Now," he said, "you must form a brotherhood of those who believe. It must be a closed community. Those who do not believe must be banished. Is your tribe wholly separate from other tribes?"

The one who spoke for the River People said, "Oh, no. We are surrounded by other tribes; we intermarry, and we're all related."

"That must stop," said the Old Man. "Separate yourselves from those who do not believe. Then those who believe will know that they belong to a precious brotherhood."

"It will be hard to do," said the representative of the River People. "We know each other quite well."

"But they don't share your faith," said the Old Man. "Therefore they are evil and must be excluded. "Those who believe must know that by virtue of believing, *they belong*. They are communicants, deeply bound to other communicants and to the faith. Those who come into the faith have come into the bosom of the faithful and are no longer alone, no longer seeking acceptance nor fearing exclusion. They are in. They are members of the church invisible."

Hardly had he finished when one of the Students spoke up: "The bloodiest pages of history are a result of the exclusivity you advocate: the we-they attitude, *we* being right, virtuous, and 'in'; *they* being wrong, evil, and outside. Maybe we're not sufficiently magnanimous to nurture our bonds with all humanity, but we can try to control our impulse to manufacture we-they relationships and to see enemies where there are none."

But the River People departed satisfied. They did not come again for some months, but when they did, they reported to the Old Man that they had formed a closed brotherhood.

The Old Man said, "Now you must have an all powerful father-figure. I do not know your tribal religion. It may be that your god or one of your gods can serve this purpose. If not, you must select one of your leaders as the Supreme One. You must fear him and abase yourself before him. Worship him. Give your troubles over to him. And understand that he is the stern, vengeful guardian of your beliefs, your doctrine, your way of life."

And the River People went away satisfied.

This time the Students did not argue with the Old Man, but as they left the meeting, they discussed the subject heatedly. "The Old Man perverts everything." said one.

"But I believe in God," said another. "Is he telling the River People anything different?"

"Yes," said the first, "something very different. He is telling them to abase themselves before *any* godlike figure. If you haven't a god, invent one. Or an all-powerful leader will do. He said nothing about an ennobling conception of the Deity, nothing about God speaking to the best in us or loving us. He said nothing about leaders of moral stature who would help us be our best selves. He is saying to the River People that they must become as frightened children before a father-figure."

When the representatives of the River People returned some months later, they reported that now they had a Supreme Leader. The Old Man praised them and said, "Now you must think about your enemies."

"But we do not have enemies," said one of them.

"Oh, yes you do!" said the Old Man. "There are those who don't share your beliefs, who don't acknowledge the authority of your Supreme Leader. They are enemies of the True Faith. There are those who worship other gods. There are people right now plotting to exploit you, or control you, or destroy you. They may even be in your midst, calling you 'Brother.' "

The River People departed to do his bidding. As the Students left, they fell to discussing the Old Man. "What you're hearing," said one of the older Students, "is a remarkably clear sketch of the ingredients of an extremist movement."

"You mean an extreme nationalist movement?"

"No," said the older Student, "*any* extremist group. A nation. A terrorist organization. An underground cell. A fanatical religious cult. An extremist guerrilla unit." Another student added, "The frightening thing is he is speaking to an impulse deep in most humans. It's so easy for us to find targets for the hostility that is in us, to believe in the existence of the enemy. Some humans seem to need objects of antagonism and paranoia. Against such enemies one may vent, in good conscience, all the hatred and venom that is suppressed in a civil community. Against beings thought to be so evil one may imagine that any act is justified—murder, torture, oppression, denial of human dignity, total withdrawal of compassion."

When the representatives of the River People next visited the Old Man, they told him they had made great progress in identifying their enemies. He praised them and said, "Now you must create a system of organized power to propagate the faith, mobilize the faithful, and combat your enemies."

"Do you mean an organized church or an army?" asked the River People.

"Both!" thundered the Old Man. This time, after the River People had left, the Students approached the Old Man. One said, "Remember, Old Man, that power often becomes an end in itself. Organizations designed to mobilize the faithful and punish backsliders often end up enslaving the faithful too."

"Your objection comes too late," the Old Man said with a mirthless smile. "I did not even need to say what I did. They would have done it anyway."

"How is that?" asked one of the Students.

"Recall the path along which I have taken them," said the Old Man. "Remember the certitude of their beliefs, the stern consequences of deviating, the pressures for loyalty, the subordination to leaders, the fear of enemies. Given all of that, they would inevitably create a system of organized power—an army, a disciplined party, a stern government."

"Of course," said one of the Students, "but you should have warned them that any system of organized power they set up must be surrounded with constitutional constraints to preserve their freedom."

The Old Man laughed. "What makes you think they won't be happy under discipline?"

One of the Students said, "We don't rule out commonly agreed-upon discipline in the service of a higher value. But you give them nothing to aspire to, no higher vision."

"My prescription is not complete," the Old Man said. "The next time I will give them the final requirement: the vision of a world totally cleansed of the evils perceived in the here and now. That is the final goal: Utopia . . . society perfected . . . humans perfected . . . a time when the Truth has come into its own and reigns unopposed. Enemies have been routed, the faith has triumphed, brotherhood has reached its perfect state. And don't tell me you don't have some such vision!"

The Students shook their heads. One of them said, "Extremism thrives on the idea that there's an earthly Utopia toward which the faithful are moving, a Utopia so gleaming that it justifies any cruelty and sacrifice on the part of those seeking to bring it about. But humans can never wholly free themselves from the flaws in their own nature. For us that is the very essence of being human and being alive. It defines our problem as humans: eternal effort to learn, but never coming to final knowledge of The Truth; eternal striving to do better but never reaching the point at which striving is no longer necessary, and imperfection is blessedly behind us."

The Old Man shook his head. "You are not like other humans."

The River People did not return for the last lesson. They had grown powerful among the River Tribes because of the fierceness of their beliefs and their discipline, and they embarked on a series of conquests that made them the unchallenged rulers of the River Country. This proved so exhilarating that they decided to attack the powerful Mountain People to the west, and, in the ensuing war, the River People were wiped out.

The Students sought out the Old Man and told him the news, adding, "You were the architect of their destruction."

The Old Man shrugged his shoulders. "Death is a form of Utopia." Then he added: "Can you honestly deny that the evil was in the River People themselves? At every step, something deep in their character responded to my counsel. And in their evil they were like all other humans."

"The impulses were in them, to be sure," said one of the older Students. "But like all other humans, there was also good in them. The only way to combat the worst in humans is to call for the best. You could have given counsel that spoke to the good."

The Old Man shrugged again. "That would require another counselor."

13 || Wholeness

Primitive man was intimately related to the world around him—the earth, the trees, the stars, the mountains, living things. Much of that world was inhabited by spirits or gods who could help or hinder him in his daily rounds. Some were friendly, some hostile, but they were all part of a great drama in which he was one of the actors. They were part of his daily life, his dreams, his religion.

Civilized man drifted away from intimacy with the natural world. Ways of thinking developed that set up dualities—man and nature, mind and body, spirit and flesh.

All too often the great world religions fostered those dualities. Many scientists strengthened the dualistic views by reacting negatively to all that could not be immediately explained in equations, thus arbitrarily cutting science off from great parts of the human experience.

The Natural World

The man-against-nature dualism permitted us to be ruthlessly destructive of the natural environment without regrets or second thoughts. The ecological crises of the twentieth century made scientists realize that they had never spent much time explaining to their nonscientific brethen how interwoven were all the things of earth.

Now we are beginning to understand. Our awareness of the pace at which we are destroying our planetary environment has had something to do with the shift. And the deeper meanings of science, filtering through the consciousness of nonscientists, have finally begun to show us that we are a part of a marvelously designed natural system that can only inspire awe.

At the same time, religious thinkers are recognizing that the world revealed by science is a worthy object of wonder and reverence; they begin to see the foolishness of rejecting science on the grounds that it is in some respects at odds with a literal interpretation of ancient texts. They are coming to see their God as the creator of the natural design that science is revealing. They are coming to see the ancient texts as products of the religious impulse expressed in terms of beliefs and imaginings then current. The same religious impulse can only express itself today in terms of today's beliefs and imaginings. It can honor the ancient strivings toward God and at the same time give free rein to the distinctive form and style of contemporary understandings and intuitions. Science has provided some of the grandest of those understandings and intuitions.

We know that we are intimately related to our physical environment. It can nurture or destroy us; we can nurture or destroy it. To say that nature is indifferent to man is meaningless. It is as though one were to say that the heart is indifferent to the thyroid gland. The concept of "indifference" is out of place. The two organs are fatefully related. The harmony and beauty of their interaction when the system is functioning well kindles awe and wonder. So it is with man and his environment when each nurtures the other.

We are not, after all, strangers to this planet. It has been our home for eons. It has had much to do with shaping us, and we have had so much to do with shaping it. It is hard to think of ourselves as in any way separable from it. We have within ourselves the elements of the earth and its atmosphere. The earth is the kind of planet it is, in part, because of the biosphere of which we are an ingredient.

This is not to accept the mystical view that we are indistinguishably merged and absorbed in the larger whole. We are not the wind nor the stars nor the forest. As humans, our outlines are distinguishable, and each of us is a person. The things in us that are uniquely human must enter into our sense of what life is or should be. Yet our species is intimately entangled not only with earth and the physical environment but with all life, all living organisms on earth. We have the same home, exhibit the same life processes, and affect one another in endless ways.

The sense of wholeness, applied in the temporal dimension, emerges as a sense of continuity. Our ancestors of 50,000 years ago were in every physical respect almost precisely like us. Their brains, their senses, their reflexes, their capacity for fear and anger, their physical response to danger—all are in us unchanged. We are the contemporary embodiment of them; they were the prefiguring of us. We are all manifestations of the same life process. We will live on in it, as Neolithic man lives on in us.

Mind and Body

As persons we are not made up of two parts—a mind and a body. It is all one. Sensory stimuli and visceral reactions affect our thinking. We cannot choose to shut out those nonrational elements; we respond with our whole being. Thoughts, acts, emotions cannot be sorted neatly into separate categories. They pervade one another.

Rationalism poses problems that merit discussion. Virtually all human history before Socrates was superstition-ridden. There were fine rational minds before Socrates, but none approached the persistence and ingenuity with which he communicated to his contemporaries the idea that we can think rationally about good and evil, about life's choices, and about means and ends. But of course Socrates also listened to his daemon, which gave him an immense advantage over some of our contemporary rationalists.

It was a good beginning, but the rise of science lent such prestige to an unqualified rationalism, that for a time, until quite recently, we allowed ourselves to be wholly imprisoned by it. We appear to be recovering. We now know that there are questions to which there are no answers in words. We know that sometimes rational explanations leave the spirit hungry. We have seen a rebellion against the narrowing and thinning out of human experience brought about by our impersonalized and "efficient" institutions. We have seen a turning away from the emphasis that large-scale organization necessarily places on rational processes and a recognition of the nonrational side of our nature, the side that involves emotion, aesthetic experience, imagination, fantasy, myths, and dreams, the side that is reached by art, poetry, drama, religion, and the continuities of tradition and of place. We have seen a revolt against the abstractions (words, numbers, indices, generalizations) intrinsic to large-scale organization and a demand for a return to immediately apprehended experience, "unprocessed reality," sensuality, and work with one's hands.

If we become so exclusively rational that the conventional framework of values leaves no room for the nonrational, then our nonrational impulses find their release outside the conventional framework—in astrology, cults, drugs, and so on. This tendency can lead to a devaluing of the rational, which makes no more sense than a devaluing of the nonrational. We must see the rational and nonrational as parts of a whole. Then the person can be whole.

14 || A Quest That Can Never End

For a year or so my writing desk was so situated that I could look out the window on a small herd of cows grazing nearby. And I must confess that the least original of all thoughts about those docile animals kept recurring to me. You never get the impression that a cow is worrying about the meaning of it all.

Humans have never been characterized by such placidity nor such indifference. All the evidence of anthropology and history tells us that humans refuse to live in a meaningless world.

Three Kinds of Meaning

There are three principal sources for the meaning that humans seek and find: science, a moral order, and religion.

The scientific impulse to understand the universe and other humans and ourselves is as natural as breathing. What we learn is useful, but even if it were not, we would go right on with our insistent inquiry. We are built that way.

Critics who attack science as a dehumanizing force will be offended to see it linked with religion and the idea of a moral order, even though the linkage involves no more than the pointing out of certain common elements. It is true that science has at times been used destructively, notably in the arms race. But science properly conceived and pursued is one of the great adventures of the mind and spirit, a means of enhancing our humanity, our sense of reverence, our oneness with the universe. Philosophers and theologians have said that the effort to bring about a union between the person and the truths and realities that lie beyond the self is at the heart of all spiritual seeking. Properly pursued, science has its place in that quest.

We also seek moral meaning: answers to all the great questions of liberty and oppression, justice and injustice, honor and dishonor. I have already commented on this human propensity. We go beyond noting the objective facts of behavior to assert that certain kinds of behavior are fitting and proper, others not. Out of such assertions we construct a moral order, supported by the authority of the community and its tradition.

The moral order is not just a conceptual system to observe or contemplate. It commands us, tells us what is expected of us, instructs us how to live. Like every other feature of society, it is subject to decay, exploitation, betrayal—and regeneration.

The third kind of meaning that humans have habitually sought and found is religious. For some, the objective truths of science aren't enough, nor is it enough to have a moral order to tell us what ought and ought not to be. They seek a framework of meaning that relates them in a deeply personal way to a Universal Order or Being (as they conceive it), that gives special significance to their lives, lends dignity to their suffering, heals the wound of separateness, and offers union with a reality larger than their own selfish concerns. (The reader will recognize that I am trying to use terms that will cover a variety of faiths.)

I asked a devoutly religious friend of mine how he would explain the human impulse to seek the three kinds of meaning: his response was simply that God designed us that way. People who do not accept religious explanations have more difficulty accounting for the insistent human search for meaning. Some dispose of the difficulty by acting as though the impulse doesn't exist. They tend to explain science on grounds of usefulness; but few great scientists really believe that. Science is useful, but the motivation that leads to the pinnacles of scientific achievement is not basically an impulse to be useful. It is something much more puzzling, not easily explained but not to be denied.

And how to explain our moral impulse? Given the manifest absence of justice in the workings of nature, given that most humans do not have an ungovernable impulse to be just, why do they insist on dreaming of a world in which justice prevails?

The three kinds of meaning are very different from one another, yet there are striking similarities among them. Each contains elements of the unknown, things beyond our grasp, things still inexplicable. Each is perceived or experienced as a reality—an Unseen Order—that exists, intangibly but powerfully, beyond the "realities" of the world we touch and see and feel. Each requires an effort on the part of the individual to relate to Objects of Value that are thought of as outside the self and larger than the self, and to accept those Objects of Value as having greater force than one's own whims and prejudices. Each in its own way requires us to take the "leap of faith." Some scientists will be uncomfortable with that statement, but as Alfred North Whitehead points out, "The restless modern search for increased accuracy of observation and for increasingly detailed explanation is based on unquestioning faith in the reign of law. Apart from such faith, the enterprise of science is foolish, hopeless."

Each of the kinds of meaning speaks to something in the individual that is beyond personally bounded motives and speaks in a commanding voice, often imposing great labors on those who believe. Each sends its believers on a quest that can never end; and to those who pursue that quest with an undivided mind, each confers the great gift of escape from self-preoccupation.

Part of our problem today—a profound part—is that we have, on the one hand, coercive societies that enchain the individual in a literal sense; and, on the other hand, free societies in which a great many individuals are enchained not by outer coercion but by the tyranny of their own restless, insatiable, hungry selves, incapable of a larger allegiance. Self-preoccupation is a prison, as every self-absorbed person finally knows. And self-pity is the most dangerous and addictive of the non-pharmaceutical narcotics.

Unfortunately, all too many of the therapeutic and personal-growth movements so popular today are essentially narcissistic. They offer no escape from the prison of the self, though they may make it possible to walk the prison yard with a lighter step.

It is easy to be cynical about any of the three kinds of meaning, since each has been abused and exploited. We have used moral codes as screens to serve our hypocrisy. We have exploited science to enhance our power. We have committed atrocities in the name of religion. But that simply says that man is imperfect. The capacity of humans to achieve the exalted goals they conceive is limited at best; but their insistence on trying is sacred. Without that effort, life is a meaningless thrashing about.

Beliefs Are Subject to Revision

Of course, the word "quest" hardly describes the attitudes of the large number of people who believe they no longer need search for the truth because they have found it. Listening to one's fellow creatures, one might conclude that certitude is the easiest thing in the world to come by. And if we are candid with ourselves, we must admit that it is a delightful intellectual shelter.

It's an especially cozy shelter when one considers cold reality: the limits of the mind itself. The mind is our only instrument for knowing: what lies beyond its power to conceptualize is forever out of reach. We can never know the extent to which the knowledge we do have is shaped by the way our minds work. Our concepts may take a certain form because our minds cannot conceive other categories. We don't even know what it is that we can never know.

One begins to understand the wisdom of Michelangelo in an ancient story. When he was painting the Sistine Chapel ceiling, a boy asked what he was doing. Michelangelo, half in jest, said, "I'm creating the noblest painting in history."

The boy said, "It doesn't look noble to me," and the artist was infuriated. "*Stolto ragazzo,*" he shouted. "Get out!" Later the chapel guard apologized for the incident but added, "You can see that the scaffolding and the cloths obscured his view. All he could see was God's fingernail. How could he grasp the whole grand design?" Michelangelo shrugged and said, "How can any of us?"

We can't know "the whole grand design". And yet humans have never let that deter them. The perimeter of the knowable is too confining for them.

Pathologies of Belief

Unfortunately, there are pathologies of belief and commitment, and we had better deal with them candidly. There is a danger of coerciveness on the part of moralists. It was not without reason that Thoreau said, "If I knew for a certainty that a man was coming to my house with the conscious design of doing me good, I should run for my life. . . ."

There is a deadly moral snobbism that says, "I'm the true patriot"; "I'm the true idealist"; "I'm the true lover of mankind"—implying that all others are counterfeit. No one who has worked with dedicated people can have failed to notice the trait. It is the enemy of wisdom. All too often reformers become so self-righteous that they develop contempt for the majority they are supposedly trying to convert, and they end up as an incestuous clique, not the least interested in moving toward a fruitful solidarity with the society.

Some individuals with inflated power drives or excessive impulses toward hatred and rage find the moral crusade an ideal vehicle to ride roughshod over others in the name of all that's true and good. Much of what appears outwardly to be the "imperiousness of the moral passions" stems from such carnivorous inner needs masquerading as virtue.

Even for those who do not have such inner needs, the

experience of combat in what is conceived to be a worthy purpose may be so exhilarating that the fighters of "the good fight" feel lifted out of themselves, transported to a higher plane of being. The sheer pleasure may be so great that almost any excuse becomes, by fiat, "a cause worth fighting for."

The worst of extremist movements stem from delusions of the undebatable rightness of "our side" and the abysmal wrongness of the opposition. Such delusions encourage separatism, exclusivity, and a paranoia that seems to justify any and all excesses of militance and violence. Thus the inevitable schismatic episodes in every extremist movement: for true zealots there is no way to disagree without parting company.

People with strong beliefs who wish to be fair in their dealings will guard against such delusions. They will know the capacity of the human mind for error and self-deception and will understand that all "truths" formulated by imperfect human beings are subject to revision.

This is not to say that we should be indifferently cordial to all views. Limitless acceptance of differing views is a luxury that can be afforded only by people who are not very serious about anything. With that caveat, we can go on to say that the humanistic tradition at its best balances many values without doctrinaire exclusion or overemphasis. It recognizes the complexity of human nature and motivation, the ambiguities of moral appraisal, the blurred edges of virtue. It counsels moderation. It sees that the tension between the needs of the individual and the group should never be wholly resolved in favor of one or the other. It knows that we're never so wrong as when we're blindly sure we're right; that at best we occasionally approximate the truth and must keep on revising; that the most deluded people are those who think they have no delusions.

15 || Problems

I began by saying that this was not a book about political or social problems in the conventional sense, that it was about attitudes and values, about motivation and morale. But after years of intense engagement with the problems of practical action, I cannot avoid all reference to the pressing challenges we face as a nation and as a species.

One of the first requirements for solving our problems is that we confront them, identify them early, appraise them honestly, and avoid complacency or evasion. We are not good at it. Humans have never been good at it. As Charlie Brown said, "No problem is so big and complicated that it can't be run away from."

The second thing to be said is that social problem solving today requires a combination of technical competence and motivated people. Experts tend to forget the latter element; idealists and zealots forget the former. When I speak of technical competence I refer to the skills of teachers and legislators as well as those of scientists and engineers.

Our limited capacity to intervene and redesign complex systems has led us into awesome errors. A social problem that appears to have been solved doesn't necessarily stay solved. Inside every solution is another problem. Our capacity to foretell the future is limited; even highly trained and sophisticated forecasters have proven themselves poor prophets.

We are still relatively unskilled in solving problems of human interaction. Our solutions are often needlessly elaborate. We overorganize, overcodify, overcontrol. We are just beginning to learn that, in social problem solving as in so many other matters, there is a simplicity that lies beyond complexity.

For all of our lifetimes the terms "problem solving" and "technology" have been inextricably linked. But in recent years technology has been in bad odor with social critics. What had been intended as servant has in too many instances become master. We would gain nothing, however, if we moved blindly to the other extreme and rejected technology (even if we could). Visions of the future are generally sketched by intellectuals, but the future also takes shape with the help of builders, traders, and makers. A view of the future that belittles the role of such people cuts itself off from great sources of human energy and ingenuity. The critics of technology forget that humans are toolmakers and builders by nature. The flint arrowhead is just as "natural" as a honeycomb or a bird's nest.

It is misleading to pass judgment on "technology" in the abstract: in the real world we are confronted by concrete and multiple "technologies." And our judgment of the social worth of any specific example must involve not only the tools but the worker and the social and physical context. Some technologies (for example, immunization against smallpox) are clearly good, some are neutral, some are clearly bad. We need technologies that are appropriate to the social, political, economic, and environmental context in which they are put to use, technologies that are designed to serve humane values.

The problems of life and society are as numberless as raindrops. They are a part of the texture of life. But if we hope to survive—and surviving, express what Elting Morison described as our best intentions toward one another—some problems loom larger than others.

At the risk of oversimplification, I'm going to suggest that we must focus on six clusters of problems.

Conflict

There is no future for the species unless we develop greater skill in dealing with the problems of human conflict. The threat of nuclear war once centered on bipolar competition between the United States and the Soviet Union. Now that fierce but clear-cut rivalry has been replaced by something infinitely more complicated, unpredictable, and dangerous: a multipolar world. No one knows what additional nations will blast their way into the nuclear club tomorrow. Every day the possibility increases that accident or miscalculation will shatter the delicate balance of fear and readiness among the nuclear powers. Worst yet, unexampled destructive power is available not only to terrorist groups but to warped or lunatic individuals. Thus we must cope not just with conflict between nations but with all human conflict, including racial and religious prejudice.

The average person thinks of peace as something passive and uneventful—a happy vacuum. If we conceive of it in that fashion, we shall never have it. We cannot abolish conflict, nor would we wish to. As a guide to a more mature conception of peace, we need only point to the conditions within any free and lawful society, where the existence of conflict is accepted as a necessary condition of social health. Conflict is not always an expression of the human impulse to violence. Sometimes it is a consequence of normal competition; sometimes it is the result of smoldering injustices that cry out for remedy. Any free and lawful society makes certain kinds of conflict possible—by encouraging the existence of a loyal opposition, by discouraging economic monopoly, by fostering freedom of expression, by empowering those who have too long been powerless.

The whole history of law and much of the history of government has been an attempt to deal in a civil fashion with human conflict, to hold it within bounds, and to resolve it peaceably within a framework of order. Thus is justice done and the peace preserved.

If we do not blow ourselves up, we shall construct a peaceful world in much the same fashion—by painstakingly putting together the institutional arrangements that permit the ebb and flow of conflict and tension within an international framework of order. After millenniums of bloodshed the goal seems unreachable, but until this century nobody really tried very hard. Certainly it is only in the last forty years that there has been a serious attempt to explore the nature of group conflict. Groups all over the world are experimenting with new forms of arbitration, tension reduction, and conflict resolution.

Every modern nation is a composite of earlier tribalisms and fierce regional loyalties, most of which have given way to national identity. With the new consciousness of our shared responsibility for our small planet, it is not inconceivable that the same process might occur worldwide. If it doesn't, then we must say our prayers.

Population

World population is increasing at the rate of 200,000 more births than deaths a day, and we shall have to endure heavy population growth for decades to come, with potentially devastating consequences in human suffering and ecological overload. No matter how hard we work at controlling fertility from this point on, a world population of considerably more than 6 billion by the year 2000 is inevitable. Since we've had no experience with that level of world population, we can't know what it will do to living conditions, food requirements, consumption of raw materials, and political balances. The burden of rapid population growth on a nation seeking economic growth is apparent. Because of the high fertility rates in the poorest countries, they might improve food production substantially and yet gain nothing—or even lose—in per capita food supply, so the nutritional level will certainly not gain, and may drop.

There has been a certain amount of fruitless debate about whether our concern over fertility rates should express itself in family-planning programs or programs of education, health, nutrition, and agricultural development. The only sensible answer is to do both. We don't know as much as we should about reducing fertility rates, but there is a good deal of evidence that they come down when the lowest income groups are lifted off the floor of absolute poverty and brought out of the utter darkness of malnutrition, ignorance, and despair.

Ecology

The revolution in environmental awareness is surely one of the great landmarks in human history. Archaeologists now tell us that mankind has been destroying one or another part of the environment for the past 10,000 years. There is evidence that soil depletion, the exhaustion of water resources, deforestation, silted waterways, and other consequences of environmental abuse occurred frequently in the ancient world—on the plains of the Indus River, in the lands of the ancient Maya, and around the Mediterranean basin, for example. Plato expressed the view that the soil erosion so evident in the Greece of his time was caused by deforestation in earlier times.

What is new is not environmental destruction itself but the scope and variety of current destruction and the extraordinary new awareness of it. We are now acutely conscious of the problems of the biosphere and the hazards to our life-support systems—the quality of our air, water, and soil, the dangers to the upper atmosphere and to the climate, the effect of man-introduced chemicals on the natural environment (including us), the thoughtless waste of nonrenewable resources. We understand in new dimensions the wisdom of Francis Bacon's aphorism, "We can command nature only by obeying her."

Some say the developed nations want pollution control at whatever cost to economic growth whereas the developing nations want economic growth at whatever cost to the environment. But that is an oversimplification. Sensible people in most nations are looking for solutions that will permit ecologically sound economic activity. We must develop (and are developing) pollution-free technologies and technologies for the prevention of pollution. We are developing energy-efficient technologies and ecologically sound agricultural methods.

We must devise better means of testing and screening the 1000 new, man-made chemicals that are introduced every year. We must learn to avoid the population overload that leads to unbearable stress on the environment. The whole world must conserve energy and nonrenewable resources. Nothing is more certain than that we will develop to far higher levels the art of recycling resources (chiefly minerals and water). With respect to soil and forests and other renewable resources, we will rebuild as we use. But some natural resources, such as oil, coal, and natural gas, are for the most part nonrecyclable and nonrenewable; the only means of conservation are more efficient use and a reduction in consumption. Today the waste of resources in the advanced countries, especially in the United States, is phenomenal and inexcusable. Clearly the industrial nations are going to have to develop an ethic of conservation. In a system based in part on the intensive stimulation of consumer wants, this will take some doing. The assumption that there will be unending availability of cheap energy is built more deeply into our way of doing things than many people realize.

The Individual and Society

The problems of the individual and society are, of course, of central importance in any serious attempt to appraise our future. But we have already discussed those problems at considerable length in earlier chapters and need not reexamine the subject here. If the

claims of society are taken to justify the snuffing out of
freedom and individuality, then the society's chief
source of creativity, vitality, and capacity for renewal
will be stifled. If, at the other extreme, individualism
disintegrates into anarchism, the outcome will be just
as grim.

Equality

It isn't necessary to review here the long history of
strivings toward equality nor the debates and struggles
that have developed in the twentieth century. The debate over equality will never end. There is no likelihood that we can make all humans equally intelligent,
equally tall, equally good, or equally happy. But we
have come to believe that we can, if we work hard at
it, make them equal before the law; that we can give
them equal opportunity; and—with considerably
greater effort—we can give them something approaching equal access to some of the crucial benefits of society, such as education, health care, shelter, and enough
to eat. If I speak cautiously, it is because I have seen too
many false and glittering promises.

We have a long, long way to go. We know the poverty
that exists in our own country. Of 2 billion people in the
roughly 100 developing nations, about 40 percent or 800
million are barely surviving. Many aren't surviving. It
is exceedingly difficult even for people who live at our
"poverty line" to understand the brutal realities of absolute poverty: mental and physical handicaps stemming from malnutrition and lack of medical care, handicaps that cripple for life, death at an early age. Under
such conditions, a phrase like "equality of opportunity"
becomes meaningless.

Values and Faith

The last cluster of problems (not last in importance) has to do with what human beings believe in and where they find meaning. Again, it is a subject we have examined at length in earlier chapters and need not review here. I would add only a brief comment on continuity and change. New values and faiths flow out of old values and faiths. The transformations may be spectacular, but they have a past. We can neither break with the past nor return to it. Life flows on. There is a Latin proverb, *Natura non facit saltum:* nature does not proceed by leaps. Still less does it leap backward. Out of its heritage of old values and faiths a vital society is always fashioning something new. If not, then the society dies at the core.

16 || Leadership

A leader is best
When people barely know that he exists
. . . Of a good leader, who talks little,
When his work is done, his aim fulfilled,
They will say, "We did this ourselves."

LAO-TSE

Such a self-effacing leader might have trouble getting reelected in our noisy and turbulent political environment. Even so, Lao-Tse's words carry wisdom.

The task of leaders in our kind of society is to help us understand the problems that all must face, to aid in the setting of goals and priorities, and to work with others in finding paths to those goals. It is part of their task to mobilize support for the goals chosen, maintaining public morale and motivation and nurturing a workable level of public unity. They must activate existing institutions in pursuit of the society's goals or, when necessary, help redesign institutions to achieve that result.

Leaders must also help people know what they can be at their best (". . . with malice toward none, with charity for all . . ."), calling for the kind of effort and restraint, drive and discipline that make for great performance. In leadership at its finest, the leader symbolizes the best in the community, the best in its traditions, values, and purposes.

In a free society, leaders perform those functions within a framework of constraints—an uncorrupted electoral process, the rule of law, institutional checks and balances, a free press. In Watergate, our nation learned bitter lessons at the hands of a president who tried to circumvent those traditional constraints. We learned again why the checks on power must be kept in working order.

The tumult of the twentieth century has retaught us the ancient lesson that people get the leaders they deserve. Good constituencies produce good leaders.

Most great (not just capable) leaders are the product of major emergencies or disasters. No doubt there are many born leaders, but it is generally only in times of trouble that we let their potentialities blossom into greatness. Great leaders—Roosevelt, Churchill, DeGaulle in our time—appear when a society needs them desperately: only under such conditions are there likely to be both the mandate and the highly motivated followers that great leadership requires. Clearly, then, no society should expect to have an endless succession of extraordinary leaders. A healthy society, especially one with our tradition of dispersed power, should be able to function well with good rather than great leaders. Indeed, one of the glories of our society is that "the system" is not excessively dependent on the leader.

But even our system can't function with fools, rascals, or nonleaders in the leadership position. We have tested the proposition. There is an unfortunate tendency in the democracies today to accept mediocre standards of performance in its leaders and then to be rather contemptuous of them. Both attitudes should be altered: we should set high standards of performance for our leaders and then honor them. A free people must create its own structure of authority and respect it.

Obstacles to Leadership

The pervasive hostility of people toward all institutions and all symbols of authority today places a heavy burden on leadership. Moreover, there is something perverse in the modern temper that seeks to diminish or destroy exemplary figures. With compulsive thoroughness we search our heroes for the hidden flaw. A now-famous political figure once said to me (before he had attained his present stature), "If the journalists encountered Adonis, they'd circle round and round him, find a pimple on his rear end, and write their stories about the pimple." The comment captures almost perfectly the obsessively vulgar spirit in which each eminent American finally gets his warts-and-all biography.

Modern journalism, especially television, needing figures larger than life, seizes on exceptional individuals and magnifies them. Ultimately, under that merciless magnification, there are no heroes, only celebrities.

Our time is rich in brilliant administrators of large-scale enterprise and able guild chiefs in one or another special field of endeavor. It has many gifted individual performers in particular fields: great scientists and artists, great surgeons and quarterbacks. But is is woefully short of broadly based leaders with the depth, dimensions, and confidence to serve the society as a whole. It lacks great teachers of the public—political leaders who are also moral leaders.

Many persons of recognized stature and power in our society seem immobilized by the gigantic, interlocking processes over which they appear to preside. One corporate chairman of my acquaintance said, "If I prepare a strong public statement, my financial vice-president faints dead away, my lawyers veto my best points, and my public relations people take all the sting out of what's left. It's like playing a game of tennis under eight feet of water."

We do not know how to create leadership gifts. But we can identify reasonably early those who have such gifts and encourage them. We can place them in proximity to proven leaders and give them a firsthand glimpse of how the society is governed. And by creating governing structures that are relatively free of corruption, we can make the leadership role attractive to gifted people. We must also try to free some of the potential leadership talent now imprisoned in specialist roles. The most valuable leaders in the years ahead will very likely be specialists turned generalists.

But the most difficult task in leadership development is to preserve a measure of creativity in the potential leader. All too often, on the long road up, young leaders become "servants of what is" rather than "shapers of what might be." In the long process of learning how the system works, they are rewarded for playing within the intricate structure of existing rules. By the time they reach the top, they are trained prisoners of the structure. This is not all bad: every vital system reaffirms itself. But ultimately no system can stay vital unless *some* of its leaders remain sufficiently independent to help it to change and grow.

17 || The Future of Freedom

The survival of freedom comes down to whether power can be held in check. Over the centuries, humans have tried many ways of achieving that end, and two strategies have emerged as far superior to all others. One is to require that power be exercised within a set of explicit and universally applicable constraints, the rule of law: one set of laws governing the strong as well as the weak, the rich as well as the poor. The other strategy is to disperse power, never allowing it to be concentrated in one person, one institution, or one group.

The barons at Runnymede had a rough grasp of both strategies, though their concept of dispersed power was somewhat limited. (The intent of the Magna Carta was that the king should share his power with the barons, not that they should share their power with the people.)

Dispersing Power

Both of the two great strategies have been studied in depth over the years. I want to comment on the dispersing of power.

One constraint on the concentration of power has been that in a majority of societies since the dawn of history, people have not accepted the finality, or sole authority, of the secular society and its institutions. R. H. Tawney, the British economic historian, spoke of

> the view of man as an amphibious being, who belongs not to one world but to two. . . . The conviction that when conscience and authority collide, it is to God, not to man, that obedience is due, finds its sanction in that conception. It is because of it that the respectable atrocities of law, custom and convention have not lacked an inner tribunal to condemn and correct them.

Denial of the finality of the society's institutions also manifests itself in secular form, most familiarly perhaps in our own arrangements through which citizens may bring about institutional revisions, including amendment of the Constitution.

The Founding Fathers were keenly aware of the desirability of dispersing power. Pit ambition against ambition, Madison advised us. Through the separation of powers, the reservation of powers to the states, and innumerable checks and balances, they made it virtually impossible for any individual or group to concentrate power in one place.

In addition, all the industrial democracies have a private sector that serves as crucially important insurance that government will not be all-powerful. In fact, over the centuries in the Western world one or more groups outside government—the church, commercially powerful groups, a landowning class, corporations, guilds or unions, political parties and professions have at times had power rivaling—or exceeding—that of government itself. So holding power accountable includes scrutinizing not just the government itself but any organized groups and institutions within the society that have proven their capacity, if unchecked, to coerce other segments of the society (or to exercise *sub rosa* control of government itself).

It is wrong to suppose that a free and informed electorate can easily override such concentrations of power. Clearly it can be enormously effective if the electoral process remains reasonably uncorrupted. But one discovers that the power of the voters expressing their views one by one is too broadly and thinly spread to match the power of organized groups, which have ways other than the ballot to influence government.

In the nineteenth century, the institutions of private capitalism became far too powerful and often wielded their power irresponsibly, leading to the popularity of the proposal that the state—in theory representing the people—should take over capitalistic institutions. It was an understandable reaction against power that seemed beyond the reach of accountability on any other terms.

But after observing totalitarian governments that have taken over capitalistic enterprise, even convinced critics of capitalism have come to see that such power concentrated in government can be as dangerous as concentrations of power in the private sector. They have come to recognize anew the importance of dispersion of power and the virtues of a vigorous nongovernmental sector.

The United States and the other democratic industrial nations have preserved a vital nongovernmental sector but have repeatedly taken governmental action to curb the abuse of power by private organizations and groups (corporations, unions, professions, and so on). In the process we have discovered that dispersing power is an endless task. (It never stays dispersed for long.) The problem is complicated by the fact that the instrument for maintaining a system of dispersed power—the government—itself tends to accumulate and concentrate power. So we are faced with a balancing act. How can we keep the nongovernmental sector free and vigorous and creative? When concentrations of power in that sector become so great and so abusive as to endanger our liberties, how can we set constraints without making government itself excessively powerful?

Anyone who expects a definitive answer to such questions is naïve. We're still learning.

We have learned that although the best-known totalitarian societies of our day have strong ideological bases for their coercive style, every one of them was helped to power by the political and social disarray that preceded the takeover. When one sees unchecked corruption, rampant injustice, freedom to the point of license, and all the other forces that destroy political integrity and undermine values, one may be sure that coercion is waiting in the wings. The coercive state is the receivership of bankrupt social systems.

The Totally Programmed Community

In a recent lecture I discussed the ideas presented here, and afterward a member of the audience told me I was talking about a choice between freedom and totalitarianism that was no longer before us. He said I wasn't facing the fact that the next phase will resemble neither the untidy free societies of today nor the equally untidy totalitarian societies. The next phase, he asserted, will bring the abolition of individuality, totally programmed communities, genetic engineering, and behavior modification to produce a planned result. He assured me that he abhorred such a future, but that it was coming because we are too stupid to control population, conserve resources, protect our planetary environment, and abstain from nuclear wars. Our stupidity, he told me, would lead to unimaginable catastrophes, and out of the catastrophes would arise a totally regimented society.

One cannot reject the argument lightly. Our stupidity is demonstrable, catastrophes could occur, and the potentialities for regimentation are obvious. We have learned that through social conditioning the mind can be manipulated. The person turns out not to be inviolable. One can conceive of the day when cleverly contrived social arrangements will absorb all individuality, and the very concept of self will vanish. Such nightmare visions are a modern staple.

Yet I do not believe that such a society is imminent; nor am I prepared to accept the assumption that it would be overpoweringly strong once established. Every prophecy I have read of the totally programmed society has left me with a profound impression of its vulnerability—to decay, to unforeseen changes in environing conditions, to attack by dissident elements that have retained their flexibility and capacity to improvise.

Every step toward the totally programmed society is a step away from versatility and inventiveness. How could one keep a measure of creativity, imagination, and improvisation in leaders who have been genetically selected and culturally programmed for certain roles and certain kinds of behavior? How could they handle an unforeseen emergency that required different roles and other kinds of behavior? Such a society could come into being but could not survive. It would experience a swift descent into arteriosclerosis.

People who are fearful of such a society say, "Yes, but it would eradicate or brainwash all dissenters. Who would be left to oppose it?" The view implicit in the question reckons without the intrinsic weaknesses of the Organization, and the explosive hidden strength of the person. The Organization may overwhelm, en- slave, brainwash, depersonalize. It may totally suppress individual expression. It may shape people who be- have, dress, speak, and think in precisely prescribed ways. As Heinrich Heine put it (in 1842), "Perhaps there will be only one flock and shepherd with an iron staff and a flock of human sheep all shorn alike and bleating alike!"

But we now know enough about the diseases of large- scale organization to know that the Ultimate Pro- grammed Society will have vulnerabilities stemming from its very rigidity, its suppression of criticism, and its incapacity to improvise. And it will never enjoy the certainty that it has banished forever the dangerous seeds of human contrariness. Sooner or later, behind one of those identical uniforms and masklike conform- ing faces, old, irrepressible human traits will stir omi- nously: rebelliousness, the capacity to doubt, a vagrant imagination, and a volatility of aspiration—the qualities that lend an unpredictable, troublesome, and often beautiful quality to human behavior.

Some people appear to have none of those qualities in significant measure. But somewhere among any group of humans, however sternly trained in conformity, the qualities are there, like seeds lying dormant. The seed, weak and apparently inconsequential, lodges in a tiny crevice of the solid stone. Then it sprouts, sends roots deep into the crevice, and cracks the stone. How many tyrants have sought and failed to destroy that hidden seed!

18 || Renewal

Most civilizations we know anything about have had a life span: Sumer, Egypt, Greece and Rome, the Mayan civilization, and so on. They come into being; they flourish, or at least survive, for a time; they decay; they die.

There is validity in the widespread apprehension today. An era is ending. We are leaving a familiar world behind. But that doesn't necessarily mean that our civilization is dying; there are many peaks and valleys in the long life span of a civilization. A new era lies ahead. If we can do something, even a little, to shape it to our purposes and values, we must pursue the possibility.

To think clearly about it, one must first recognize that a healthy society is one in which, at any given time, some things are being born, some things are flourishing in maturity, and some things are dying. At the time of World War I, the horse-drawn buggy was headed for extinction; railroads were in their prime; air and automobile travel were in their infancy. Innovation, decay, death, and renewal occur in parallel, affecting different parts within the system. So it is in the human body. At any given moment, some cells are dying, some are coming into being. So it is with plants in a garden. In a vital society, the forces making for disintegration and death are balanced—or more than balanced—by new life, growth, and health.

Continuity and Change

Renewal involves both continuity and change. The continuity of the generations and of tradition make possible change that doesn't descend into chaos or veer wildly in catastrophic directions. Even in these times of swift change there are more continuities intact and vital than the prophets of disintegration are inclined to admit. Indeed many of our rebels would be embarrassed to learn how much they themselves are a product of those continuities. For example, when angry dissenters form a committee and speak out critically, they think of themselves chiefly as agents of change, and they may prove to be so; but they are also products of an American tradition of dissent by self-nominated citizen groups—a tradition that has its roots in our colonial period.

Just as continuities are inescapable, change is inevitable. Even conserving involves change. The deep-sea fisherman who ventures far afield for new fishing grounds is not interested in change for the sake of change; he seeks change in the service of continuity. It is often true that the only way to conserve is to innovate, that the only stability is stability in motion. No society has the option to forgo change. The question is whether it can make change serve its continuing purposes and values.

The instinct of humans to stabilize their environment, both outer and inner, leads them inevitably to invest their customs and social arrangements with a sense of permanence, of sacredness, of unchallengeable *rightness*. The human need for stability leads over the years to an institutional rigidity that is essentially antinature. Nature is always in flux, moving, changing. Things are being born, maturing, adapting, competing, surviving, dying.

Humans create organizations and societies to serve their shared purposes and then gradually rigidify those institutions as though in a vain attempt to shut out the tumult of nature. But nature wins. Eventually, in trying to escape the great ebb and flow of life, societies and organizations smother themselves. Then the human spirit escapes and moves on to create new forms and, over centuries, to build new prisons from which it must again escape.

The Villain Within

Almost no one is hostile, in principle, to the idea of renewal. Then why is it so difficult to effect? Part of the problem is that decay starts from within. When individuals close their minds, stop learning, become set in their ways, it is not as a rule because anyone forced them to do so. So it is with nations: generally nations aren't pushed by external forces into senility and oblivion; rather, they die of internal decay.

In short, one must look for the villain within—within oneself, within one's society—a process no one really enjoys. Thus critics who tell us what our trouble is may be fiercely resented. It isn't that people can't find the path that will save them. They run from it. They cry, "Where is the voice that will tell us the truth?" and clamp their hands over their ears. They shout "Show us the way!" and shut their eyes.

Those who understand what we must do in order to stave off self-destruction are unwelcome because they tell us to rearrange things within ourselves or our society that we have no intention of rearranging. There's nothing more irritating than a savior when you're not ready to be saved.

Obstacles to Renewal

The status quo is a fabric not easily unraveled. There are precedents, traditions, customs, written codes, and unwritten rules—some still useful, and others the petrified remains of what was once useful. There are procedures, techniques, methods, and standards, some still sound, some long outworn. There are arrangements that cannot easily be changed because to change them would alter the distribution of power or wealth. There are institutions that cannot be overhauled because their long existence has conferred on them a certain sanctity.

In any society, over time, form triumphs over spirit. We create institutions to serve us and let them become prisons that incarcerate us. The artist can become a prisoner of his style. The civilization becomes trapped by its greatest achievements. Established individuals become less adventurous because they have reputations to preserve. People cannot break new paths because they have prior commitments and obligations. Possessions possess. All the comfortable, known things that make for emotional security stand between us and the hazards of the unknown. The human being, greatest of all generalists, moves toward a specialization that limits individual growth.

It is generally thought that intellectuals speak for change, but this is not consistently true. There are intellectuals, including radical intellectuals, who speak for dying institutions. Indeed, at any given time parts of the intellectual world are dying, and the intellectuals involved may be the last to recognize it.

Conditions Favoring Renewal

Highly motivated people easily break the bonds of outworn practices. In contrast, individuals low in motivation accept the constraint of aging institutions. That is why the draining away of hope and trust leads inevitably to decay.

The same principle operates with respect to attitudes about the future. People with a buoyant view of the future are unlikely to be trapped in obsolete arrangements. People preoccupied with the past or despairing about the future are likely to welcome the seeming security of moribund institutions. In the words of the old couplet, they won't let go of nurse for fear of something worse.

Within the aging society there is a rigid compartmentalization that blocks communication among groups—perhaps between rulers and ruled, or between higher and lower economic strata, or among racial, religious, and other subgroups. Communication among diverse elements is the first condition of creativity. It can only occur when there is a certain flexibility of internal structure. The ancient obstacle to such internal flexibility was the existence of rigid caste and class barriers. The modern obstacle is specialization, by far the most important barrier to internal communication within a society.

Diversity and Dissent

As the times and the environment change, even a very successful society may have to seek new solutions. So just as a species has in the genes of its members a great storehouse of possibilities for future adaptation, a society must have within itself a range of alternatives for possible future use. Pluralism, dissent, and the free market of ideas not only test the validity of contemporary doctrine but build an inventory of possible alternative solutions. These are a society's seedbeds. That is one of many reasons why a society must contain a range of human types—scientists and artists, doers and dreamers, wanderers and stay-at-homes—representing many divergent points of view.

People who despise conventionality are apt to regard our contemporary society as mired in conformity, but we have seen in recent years an unprecedented volume and variety of intellectual and social experimentation—religious movements, psychological doctrines, philosophical experiments, new patterns of living, new assumptions, new vocabularies. No sensible person either accepts or rejects them all uncritically.

Unfortunately, even dissenters become set in their ways. Some speak for ideas that once were revolutionary but are not so any longer. Some forms and expressions of dissent have become so rigid, stylized, and traditional that they are no more capable of bringing vitality to the society than is a moribund status quo.

Freedom to experiment, consider alternatives, and dissent is not to be confused with a self-indulgent, "anything goes" approach to life. Major social renewals have rarely been associated with license. Groups at the forefront of historical social change have generally been characterized by a certain austerity. People cannot gain command of events until they gain command of themselves.

The Capacity for Regeneration

The powerful bonds of custom, habit, and institutional rigidity often form a seemingly impenetrable barrier to renewal. But the human capacity for renewal is also powerful. It may become imprisoned by institutional forms, layered over by hypocrisy, betrayed by power brokers who exploit it for their purposes. But one day the spirit reasserts itself, breaks through the smothering layers, sweeps aside institutional impediments, and releases the primordial vitality without which everything dies. The spirit "that giveth life" resides in individuals, not in organizations.

19 || A New Hard-bitten Morale

When the regeneration of societies has been achieved, as it often has been over the course of history, the agents of that achievement have been people with the capacity to hope. It is worth reflecting on where we stand today with respect to that attribute.

No doubt at certain points in our history we have suffered from a habit of shallow optimism. More recently, that juvenile optimism has been succeeded in some quarters by an equally juvenile defeatism—a gloom that is fashionably sophisticated and, like self-pity, curiously satisfying. But along the historical and evolutionary trail, defeatism has proven a poor companion. The species has been sustained through the ordeals of life on earth by a stubborn vitality that swept aside defeatism.

Among the people who express the greatest cynicism and disillusionment today is what one might call the crypto-Utopian. Hidden beneath the layers of bitterness and defeatism is a yearning soul that believes man and society to be perfectible and is outraged that we have fallen so far short.

In truth, the crypto-Utopians have a marvelously self-indulgent game going. If you expect perfection and will settle for nothing less, you can scorn the efforts of imperfect men and women to achieve what turns out to be less than perfection. You can feel wise and morally superior without ever getting out of your chair.

Utopianism, whether hidden or open, places an awesome burden on those who must strive to keep our imperfect society from becoming even more imperfect.

To sustain hope one need not blind oneself to reality. Surely we are sufficiently mature to admit that there isn't a solution to every problem, that we are going to fail in some of our best efforts to remedy the world's ills. We cannot weave a new social fabric overnight. The amelioration of social processes is a matter of great complexity; it is hard to judge the "right" and "wrong" of such change.

And we have deficiencies as problem solvers. We come to our responsibilities with limited wisdom, fitful courage, and a full repertory of human failings. We are not gods, and when we imagine that we are, we make fools of ourselves and bring injury to others. We cannot through organized social action meet all human needs, end all human suffering, satisfy all aspirations.

But to say there are limits to purposeful change is one thing; to give up in despair is something else. Just as we must resist the notion that we can solve everything overnight, so must we reject the notion that we can't solve anything. The view of some optimists that the world is infinitely malleable leads to bitterness and defeat. But if we go to the other extreme and prophesy that our best efforts will come to nothing, we shall never generate the force to solve our problems, and the prophecy will fulfill itself. In *War and Peace,* Prince Andrei said of Austerlitz, "We lost because we told ourselves we lost." Militarily, it wasn't that simple, but the point is clear. Fatalism saps the will. Humility is admirable, but excessive humility can paralyze. Most of the significant advances in the world have been made by people with at least a touch of irrational confidence in themselves.

All the best that humans have said and done, all that leaves us with a sense of human dignity, comes from unrelenting effort by some part of the race. And so it will be in the centuries ahead. The future is not shaped by people who don't really believe in the future. It will be built by people who see the complexities that lie ahead but are not deterred; people who are conscious of the flaws in humankind but not overwhelmed by the doubts and anxieties of life; people with the vitality to gamble on their future, whatever the odds. The element of uncertainty is not as disconcerting as one might think. Men and women of vitality have always been prepared to bet their futures, even their lives, on ventures of unknown outcome. If they had all looked before they leaped, we would still be crouched in caves sketching animal pictures on the wall.

There is a path between shallow optimism and the currently fashionable defeatism, a path that has been traveled through the centuries by men and women of sense and energy. Their sense makes them acknowledge life's grinding realities and humanity's fallibility. But their energy generates hope, as naturally and inevitably as a flame generates heat. It is not a question of philosophy. Many people with a deeply tragic view of life have still plunged into life's tasks with vitality and resolve.

Life takes strength and staying power. Stamina is an attribute rarely celebrated by the poets, but it has had a good deal to do with the history of the species. The extent to which we have it will powerfully affect our future.

Nothing is ever finally safe. Every important battle is fought and refought. Someone always has too much power, others too little. Justice is always imperiled by the unjust. We shall never resolve the healthy tensions between world-affirming and world-negating impulses.

Each generation must work to re-create the values it will live by. We cannot dream of a Utopia in which all arrangements are ideal and everyone is flawless. It is a dream of death. Life is tumultuous—an endless losing and regaining of balance, a continuous struggle, never an assured victory. That isn't a comfortable doctrine—but it accords with human experience.

We tend to imagine that earlier generations of Americans had more "character" than do our contemporaries. But the assertion is open to serious question. A good many nineteenth-and early twentieth-century Americans pursued a facile optimism that ignored life's complexities, blinded itself to human fallibilities, and assumed that nothing could ever really go wrong for America: every problem would be solved.

Those contemporary Americans from every walk of life—teachers, businesspeople, workers, artists, professionals, civil servants—who are seriously tackling the problems we face as a nation are, in important ways, more mature. They take a hardier view of life. They know there are no Utopias, that neither society nor mankind can be made perfect. They have a new hard-bitten morale that enables them to face those truths and still strive with every ounce of their energy to prevail. The new morale links the irrepressible thrust of biological vitality—hope, confidence, stamina, indomitability—with a tough-minded recognition of the limitations inherent in human planning and action. We can face up to the complexities of action and still act. We can acknowledge human fallibility and still believe in ourselves. We can do everything possible to lessen human pain and suffering without falling into the trap of imagining that life owes us freedom from pain and suffering.

We can ask no guarantees of a secure or happy future. But if we want a future that will demand the best that is in us and lend meaning to our lives, we can have it.

Index